Diverse Facets of the Effects of Facebook on Student Behaviour

Edited by

Zaved Ahmed Khan

&

Shahila Zafar

ISBN-13: 978-1983733710

ISBN-10: 1983733717

DEDICATION

To Project Based Learning (PBL) Method implemented at VIT University, Vellore

CONTENTS

ACKNOWLEDGMENTS

We wish to thank all the contributors for the enthusiasm and hard work displayed in conducting the studies.

Preface

The ability to communicate across the planet in real time has fostered new forms of social networks that never existed before. Friends can now easily stay connected despite living thousands of miles apart. The social networks we speak of today, such as Facebook, provide incredible rich communication. Pictures, audio recording, video recording, and can be freely shared by anyone with a connection to the internet. These capabilities have fostered a whole new category of social networks websites and behaviours that provide many opportunities that were never possible.

Today Facebook is considered as one of the most popular platforms for online social networking among youth, and - as many types of research show – university students. The purpose of this book is to highlight the impact of social networking sites, i.e., Facebook on students' schizotypal personality traits, social conditioning of senses, social relationships, academic performance, obsessive-compulsive disorder and leisure activities. The studies reported in the book were carried out in VIT University with regular undergraduate students in focus. These studies were a part of the project-based learning method implemented at VIT University. Under the supervision of the editors as instructors, the studies were carried out successfully and contributed towards the academic credits. However, more than just being academic requirements, the studies reveal important facets these social media on the behaviour of students in higher education as reported in the studies.

Chapter 1

Facebook and Schizotypal Personality Traits

Shounak Kanti Ghosh, Aviral Kumar, & Satyakam Mishra

Introduction

Social media as a tool to study human behavior

According to Marlene Cimons of the National Science Foundation (2010) online social networks such as Facebook or LinkedIn, already popular with millions for their easy ability to help people forge connections based on common interests, also have become ideal "laboratories" for social scientists who want to study human behavior. Data available from online networks can provide insights into certain behaviors—how people will vote in upcoming elections, for example, or what consumer products they are likely to buy—and also can prompt blueprints for engineering new social systems, and predicting certain events and economic outcomes. "The volume of online social networking is exploding, and it appears it is becoming more pervasive than real-life social networking," said Dan Stefanescu, professor of mathematics and computer science at Suffolk University in Boston, where he is directing several projects using online social networks as a research tool to study human behaviour. This is not surprising, given the ease with which one can pursue interactions in the digital world.

Furthermore, in an online social network environment, "it is so much easier to find new 'friends' for social intercourse because, unlike in real life, one can reach the 'friends' of 'friends' of 'friends' of your 'friends,' ad infinitum," he added. Social network introduces an individual to a variety of ideas and shapes our thoughts. In many cases, it is known to have given an online identity to a person that is drastically different from his real-life identity allowing varied expression of thoughts and interaction amongst people. Hence social media is tremendously interrelated to a person's thoughts and behavior.

The growth of Facebook and its negative effects

Facebook has been criticized for making people envious and unhappy due to the constant exposure to positive yet unrepresentative highlights of their peers. Most users of Facebook usually only display the positive aspects of their lives while excluding the negative.

Envy has profound effects on other aspects of life and can lead to severe depression, self-loathing, rage and hatred, resentment, feelings of inferiority and insecurity, pessimism, suicidal tendencies and desires, social isolation, and other issues that can prove very serious. This condition has often been called "Facebook Envy" or "Facebook Depression" by the media. Research performed by psychologists from Edinburgh Napier University indicated that Facebook adds stress to users' lives. Causes of stress included fear of missing important social information, fear of offending contacts, discomfort or guilt from rejecting user requests or deleting unwanted contacts, the displeasure of having friend requests rejected or ignored and having to use appropriate etiquette for different types of friends. It has been admitted by many students that they have faced bullying on the site, which leads to psychological harms. When that self is then broken down by others by badmouthing, criticism, harassment, criminalization or vilification, intimidation, demonization, demoralization, belittlement, or attacking someone over the site it can cause much of the envy, anger, or depression. People would like to believe they can see themselves through the eyes of others, and Facebook allows them to do that, according to a Harvard study and survey of students. People become used to thinking and doing everything in front of an audience. As their every thought is put up online for their "friends" to see, they get used to behaving in front of a crowd.

Employers are less than satisfied with the face-to-face communication skills of recent graduates according to allbusiness.com. The social networking site of Facebook does not allow for active communication. Professor Craig Fox of the philosophy department is worried that the shorter attention-grabbing bursts of communication on Facebook could be taken as a detrimental model for all communications. Facebook also takes the expressions and emotions out of communicating. Instead of meeting in person, many people choose to virtually chat with friends, family members, and even employers on Facebook's instant messenger or comment section.

Schizotypal personality traits

Personality disorders are long-standing patterns of maladaptive behavior. People with schizotypal personality disorder are often described as odd or eccentric and usually have few if any, close relationships. They don't understand how relationships form or the impact of their behavior on others. They may also misinterpret others' motivations and behaviors and develop a significant distrust of others. These problems may lead to severe anxiety and a tendency to turn inward in social situations, as the person with schizotypal personality disorder responds inappropriately to social cues and holds peculiar beliefs.

This study is aimed at connections between the attitudes of people toward the social networking platform Facebook, their views and beliefs regarding common conspiracy theories and their scores on measures of schizotypy. This will then be integrated into the schizotypy assessment, linking the attitudes toward conspiracy theories and perceptions of surveillance with scores on common personality measures and their mood, self-concept and interpersonal relationship

Methodology

Sampling and Data Collection

This descriptive study was conducted using a survey method. The population comprised of students of the age group 16-20 years from various schools and universities. A questionnaire was created, and a survey was taken online with help from Survey Monkey at the following link:

http://www.surveymonkey.com/s.aspx?PREVIEW_MODE=DO_NOT_USE_THIS_LINK_FOR_COLLECTION&sm=ZFY5nx13a4wk%2f%2bPdaJ0%2b1BWNi1cpYRpHPYBxmKOWbAA%3d .

The questions were borrowed from an ongoing survey by the University of Westminster, London, UK. Their survey which is far more elaborate can be found at the following link:

https://westminsterpsych.az1.qualtrics.com/SE/?SID=SV_b8b77oUI7aKtkhe

The responses selected were limited to 100 students who were from different institutions. The study was limited only to the attitudes and actions of people on Facebook and perception of surveillance with scores on common personality measures.

Data Analysis Techniques

The questions were framed, and feedbacks were received, and a descriptive analysis of the data received was obtained through surveymonkey.com

Results and Discussion

Based on previous research by Lankton and McKnight (2011) attitudes and beliefs with regard to the interaction with a social networking platform is assessed regarding how much participants trust this form of technology. The following, Table 1, made out of the responses indicates a considerable percentage of respondents (~25%) interact with Facebook like any other living body. Even though it is a platform for social networking, subconsciously or consciously people associate with it, and it becomes such an integral aspect of their lives that they start attributing features of living entities to it. This indicates an emotional dependence on Facebook in which they might start seeking temporary emotional refuge, cutting them off from the rest of the world.

Table 1 shows a majority of respondents agree that they feel they are constantly being monitored by Facebook but only around 10% attribute Facebook to be like traits of a living person. However, 25% interacts with Facebook as if they are interacting with a real person.

	Strongly Disagree	Disagree	Neither Agree nor Disagree	Agree	Strongly Agree	Total
When interacting with Facebook, I would feel like interacting with a real person.	8.22% 6	36.99% 27	26.03% 19	24.66% 18	4.11% 3	73
It sometimes feels like Facebook monitors what I am doing.	6.85% 5	26.03% 19	21.92% 16	39.73% 29	5.48% 4	73
I can imagine Facebook to be a living creature.	45.21% 33	31.51% 23	13.70% 10	9.59% 7	0% 0	73
I often think that Facebook is a real person.	49.32% 36	30.14% 22	15.07% 11	4.11% 3	1.37% 1	73
Sometimes Facebook seems to have real feelings.	49.32% 36	26.03% 19	13.70% 10	9.59% 7	1.37% 1	73

Table 1- Dependence on Facebook

	Very Inaccurate	Moderately Inaccurate	Neither Inaccurate nor Accurate	Moderately Accurate	Very Accurate	Total
Am the life of the party	12.33% 9	16.44% 12	30.14% 22	31.51% 23	9.59% 7	73
Sympathize with others' feelings	0% 0	5.48% 4	12.33% 9	45.21% 33	36.99% 27	73
Have frequent mood swings	19.18% 14	15.07% 11	20.55% 15	26.03% 19	19.18% 14	73
Have a vivid imagination	4.11% 3	5.48% 4	10.96% 8	36.99% 27	42.47% 31	73
Don't talk a lot	23.29% 17	13.70% 10	17.81% 13	24.66% 18	20.55% 15	73
Am not interested in other people's problems	17.81% 13	28.77% 21	30.14% 22	13.70% 10	9.59% 7	73
Often forget to put things back in their proper place	13.70% 10	19.18% 14	27.40% 20	28.77% 21	10.96% 8	73
Am relaxed most of the time	8.22% 6	15.07% 11	13.70% 10	38.36% 28	24.66% 18	73
Have difficulty understanding abstract ideas	35.62% 26	30.14% 22	16.44% 12	12.33% 9	5.48% 4	73
Get upset easily	17.81% 13	35.62% 26	10.96% 8	21.92% 16	13.70% 10	73
Feel others' emotions	2.74% 2	8.22% 6	23.29% 17	32.88% 24	32.88% 24	73
Like order	10.96% 8	6.85% 5	27.40% 20	26.03% 19	28.77% 21	73

Table 2- Emotional responses and Facebook

Schizotypy is associated with poor social functioning. The results in Table 2 show that a number of people are apathetic towards social situations and problems faced by other people. Their emotional threshold is also lower than others, and they get upset easily. About 34% agree to this. They are also susceptible to frequent mood swings (35%). Also, communication becomes limited to the real world due to extensive cyber interactions.

The responses in Table 3 suggest that a similar number of people experience varying levels of social anxiety and interpret usual everyday situations differently and attach a special meaning to them. This is indicative of schizotypal behavioural traits. Furthermore, their belief in clairvoyance and telepathy reinforces their odd behavioral patterns. The responses also indicate the prevalence of paranoia and insecurity in social situations. Majority of respondents agree that they remain aloof and prefer to keep to themselves.

	Yes	No	Total
Do you sometimes feel that things you see on the TV or read in the newspaper have a special meaning for you?	67.65% 46	32.35% 22	68
I sometimes avoid going to places where there will be many people because I will get anxious.	33.82% 23	66.18% 45	68
I have little interest in getting to know other people.	36.76% 25	63.24% 43	68
People sometimes find it hard to understand what I am saying.	54.41% 37	45.59% 31	68
People sometimes find me aloof and distant.	52.94% 36	47.06% 32	68
I prefer to keep to myself.	70.59% 48	29.41% 20	68
I am mostly quiet when with other people.	48.53% 33	51.47% 35	68
I rarely laugh and smile.	10.29% 7	89.71% 61	68
Do you believe in clairvoyancy (psychic forces, fortune telling)?	27.94% 19	72.06% 49	68

Do you believe in clairvoyancy (psychic forces, fortune telling)?	27.94% 19	72.06% 49	68
I often hear a voice speaking my thoughts aloud.	47.06% 32	52.94% 36	68
I find it hard to be emotionally close to other people.	25% 17	75% 51	68
My "non-verbal" communication (e.g. smiling and nodding during conversation) is poor.	17.65% 12	82.35% 56	68
Have you often mistaken objects or shadows for people, or noises for voices?	23.53% 16	76.47% 52	68
I am sure I am being talked about behind my back.	58.82% 40	41.18% 28	68
Do you believe in telepathy (mind-reading)?	50% 34	50% 34	68
Have you ever had the sense that some person or force is around you, even though you cannot see anyone?	35.29% 24	64.71% 44	68

Do you ever get nervous when someone is walking behind you?	26.47% 18	73.53% 50	68
I sometimes forget what I am trying to say.	64.71% 44	35.29% 24	68
Have you ever noticed a common event or object that seemed to be a special sign for you?	54.41% 37	45.59% 31	68
Do you feel that there is no-one you are really close to outside of your immediate family or people you can confide in or talk to about personal problems?	32.35% 22	67.65% 46	68
I am poor at returning social courtesies and gestures.	30.88% 21	69.12% 47	68
Have you had experiences with astrology, seeing the future, UFOs, ESP or a sixth sense?	30.88% 21	69.12% 47	68

Table 3- Schizotypal behavioural traits and Facebook

Conclusion

It is concluded from this study, that a small percentage of people using Facebook are developing varied symptoms of schizophrenia in urban Indian population. It occurs at every age, but shows marked differences in its core symptoms and consequences in the early onset of adolescence. The fact above and the disorder itself can be adequately understood if certain biological and environmental factors taken into account, the range of available mental responses, the individual conditions at illness onset and the overall cultural and socio-economic context. According to social defeat theory, the long-term exposure leads to sensitization of the dopamine system and or to increase baseline activity of this system, thereby to an increased risk for schizotypal personality traits. The present study has several limitations. First, the sample is small. There are small group differences based on sex composition, although we controlled for this in data analysis. Another limitations concern generalization of findings related to general traits.

References

Abbott, G.Byrne, L.K (2013), Schizotypal traits are associated with poorer identification of emotions from dynamic stimuli-*Psychiatry Research* (207). 40-44.

Arzy.S, Mohr C, Molnar, Szakacs.I, Blanke (2011), the Schizotypal perceptual aberration of time: Correlation between score, behaviour and brain activity-*PLoS ONE* 6(1), Article no. 1615.

Aguirre F, Sergi M.J, Levy C.A (2008), Emotional intelligence and social functioning in persons with schizotypy –*Schizophrenia Research* 104(1-3), 255-264

Bora, E., Baysan A., L.(2009). Effect of age and gender on schizotypal personality traits in the normal population, *Psychiatry and Clinical Neurosciences* 63(5), 663-669

Hafner, K. Maurer, W an der Heiden (2103), ABC Schizophrenia study: An overview of results since 1996-*Soc Psychiatry Psychiatr Epidemiol* (48):1021-1031.

Karcher. N, Shean.G (2012), Magical ideation, schizotypy and the impact of emotions-*Psychiatry Research* 197(1-2), 36-40.

Kim M-S, Hong M-H, Choi D.B (2011), Neuropsychological profile of college students with schizotypal traits- *Comprehensive Psychiatry* 52(5), 511-516.

Lahti, J., Veijola, J., Järvelin, M., Räikkönen, K., Sovio, U., Miettunen, J., Hartikainen, A-L., Pouta, A., Tanila, A., Joukamaa, M., (2009), Early life origins of schizotypal traits in adulthood - *British Journal of Psychiatry* 195(2), 132-137

Luis H. Ripoll, Jamil Zaki, Maria Mercedes Perez-Rodriguez, Rebekah Snyder, Kathryn Sloan Strike, Ayelet Boussi, Jennifer A. Bartz, Kevin N. Ochsner, Larry J. Siever (2013), Empathic accuracy and cognition in schizotypal personality disorder- *Psychiatry Research* (12), 210- 218.

McCleery, A., Divelbiss, M., St-Hilaire, A., Aakre, J.M, Seghers, J.P, Bell E.K (2102), Predicting social functioning in schizotypy: An investigation of the relative contributions of theory of mind and mood- *Journal of Nervous and Mental Diseases* 200(2), 147-152

Morgan Clifford, T., King Richard, A., Weiss John, R., John, S., (2008), *Introduction to Psychology.* New Delhi: Tata McGraw Hill Publishers

Nelson, M.T, Seal, M. L, Pantelis, C., Philip, L.J (2013), Evidence of a dimensional relationship between schizotypy and schizophrenia: A systematic review-*Neuroscience and Biobehavioral Reviews* (37), 317-127.

Chapter 2

Social Conditioning of Tastes, Behaviour, and Preferences by Peers on Facebook

Debayan De Bakshi, Sai Somesh, & Rajarshi Chakraverty

Introduction

Peer Influence has always been an inarguable factor in a person's decision-making process. As human beings took up the mantle of a "social animal" they formed communities and various social groups with which they could identify. The result was simple; mobilisation of mass opinion towards specific tastes and patterns. The best example of this would be brand loyalty and allegiance to products like Coke, Apple, Nike and so on. Till the advent of social networking, the one-way dissemination and advertisement by Producers was an accepted norm in marketing, publicity, and modulation of Consumer palates.

Today, social networks, such as Facebook, promote vibrant and novel forms of social dialogue, ideation, and collaboration. Social networking sites bestow upon the users a unique advantage of being able to update, participate and initiate discussions at the click of a button while sharing their wider interests. From general repartee to propagating breaking news, from scheduling an exam to following election results and synchronizing disaster response, from gentle humour to serious research, social networks are now used for a host of different reasons by various user communities. Hence, in this vastly public forum, a private palate was also being served. The homogeneity of social networks is one of the most striking regularities of group life (1–4). Across numerous social situations— from secondary school to college, the workplace to the household (5–8)—and with respect to a wide variety of personal attributes— from substance abuse to religious beliefs, political sympathies to tastes in food (1, 6, 9, 10)—friends tend to be much more alike and comparable than chance alone would envisage. Two mechanisms are most commonly cited as explanations. First, friends may be similar due to social selection or homophily: the tendency for like to attract like or similar people to befriend one another (11, 12). Second, friends may be similar due to peer influence or diffusion: the tendency for characteristics and behaviours to spread through social ties such that friends increasingly resemble one another over time (13, 14). Though many prior studies have attempted to untangle these two mechanisms, their respective significance is still poorly understood.

The change in medium of peer influence is evident. Instead of entrepreneurs endorsing their products or political parties trying to propagate their views, the advent of the "Facebook Friend" was observed. The Facebook Friend was a personal contact whose views impacted us more than advertisements. The reason was that of intimate trust, and they want to be accepted. In today's modern world a "like", "share" or "comment" replaced the hug or a pat on the back. Greater visibility of such actions to fellow peers by usage of the internet prompted a new age of peer conditioning.

Our experiment aims to see how far reaching peer influence via Facebook is. We shall stratify the questionnaire into various gradations of importance. It shall progress from simple lifestyle choices like movie decisions to more profound and personal ones like voting and social consciousness. Therefore, the independent variable is peer influence, and the dependent variable is the resulting behaviour, tastes, and preferences. As an example, about one-third of a million more people showed up at the ballot box in the United States in 2010 because of a single Facebook message on Election Day (15). Hence, it would not be unfair to assume that similar important real-world behaviour in the Indian context should be possible.

The subjects having an active Facebook account will be randomly selected from VIT to whom online, and hardcopy questionnaires will be provided. Answers will be completely anonymous. Statistical parameters will be decided as the questionnaire is formed and the responses are being analysed.

Methodology

The data were randomly collected from 120 students at VIT University, Vellore with the help of surveymonkey.com. The following hypotheses were considered:

Null hypothesis (Ho): Heavy peer influence via Facebook for Lifestyle preferences, Consumer Tastes and Individual decision making and Opinions.

Alternative hypothesis (Ha): Facebook independent for Lifestyle preferences, Consumer Tastes and Individual Decision making and Opinions.

Results and Discussion

Figure 1- Gender and Facebook usage

On further analysis of our data, we realised that there was major subdivision; that of gender. We scrutinized the questions regarding a number of Facebook friends, duration of active account and period of usage. These three questions (3, 4, 5) despite giving us broad segregations and validating our assumptions for the age group (18 to 22 years) taken into consideration, were not relevant to our study as they showed too much variation and no correlation with our hypothesis. For example, we look at question 5.

Question 8: How do you hear about new music?

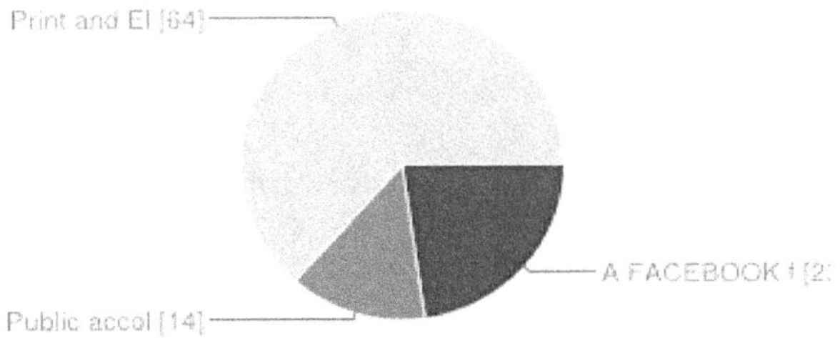

Figure 3- Awareness of new music

The majority of the subjects chose option 3 (Print and Electronic media besides Facebook) followed by option 1(A Facebook friend had posted/shared about the new artist/genre) and finished by option 2 (Public accolades/criticism via updates in Trending section of Facebook.) This shows that for personal tastes like music or food we tend to go with our likings followed by that of our peers and friends. Abstract advertisements or nonhuman influences have a minimized effect on us. Males and Females exhibit similar taste patterns.

CONSUMER PREFERENCES:

Question 11: How do you choose a brand for your electronic gadgets?

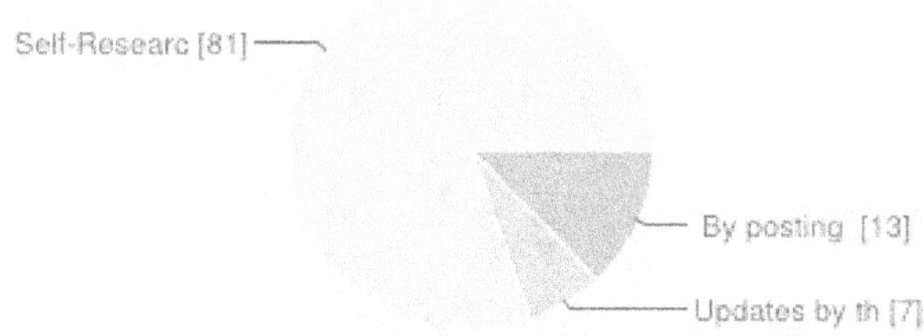

Figure 3- Medium for choosing gadgets

The response in a similar vein was observed in the category of Consumer Preferences for electronic gadgets and other products (books, clothes and so on). A person's lifestyle choices tend to be based on self-curation and customized choices. They are least bothered by the influences of Facebook regarding peer posts of brand advertisement.

7	Option 1	male	question 11
3	Option 2		
50	Option 3		
5	Option 1	Female	
4	Option 2		
31	Option 3		

Table 2- Consumer preferences gender wise

Males and Females exhibit similar consumer preference patterns.

Behaviour:

Question 20: for the General Elections of 2014 has your opinion on whom to vote for being molded most by-

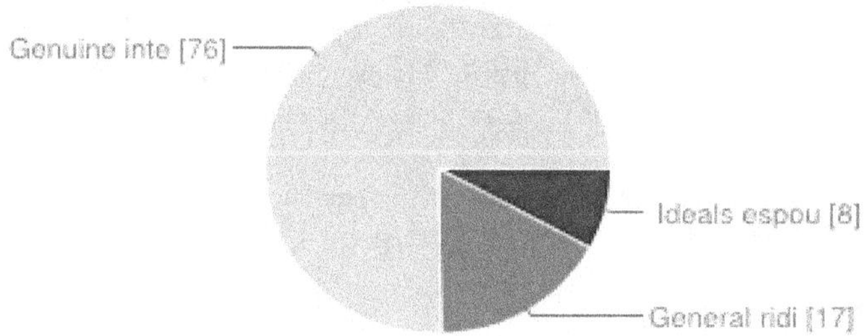

Figure 4- Voting in General Elections 2014

The age group under consideration seems to be more expressive and wants to get involved in the matters of national importance. i.e., no direct personal effect on the life of the individual. A good example would be the recent trends in statuses put up by the youth for or against political parties and urging the populace to vote. Similar to the preference and tastes, behaviour on social networking platforms depends on distinctive ideas and opinions and not on herd mentality.

4	Option 1	male	question 19
10	Option 2		
46	Option 3		
3	Option 1	female	
7	Option 2		
30	Option 3		

Table 3- Voting patterns gender wise

Males and Females exhibit similar behaviour patterns.

Question 13-How do you decide your Sports Allegiances (Individuals, Clubs or Nations)?

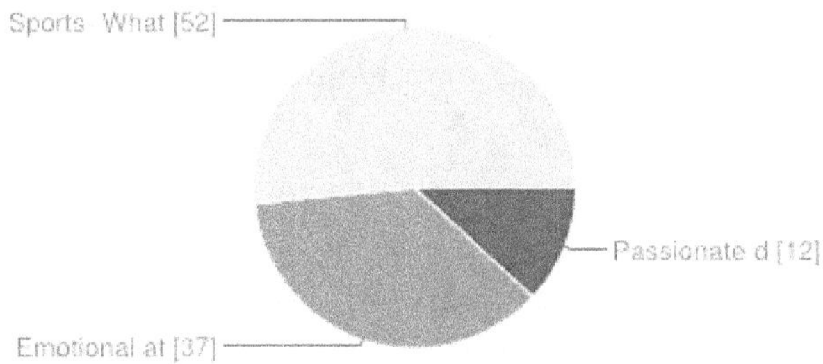

Figure 5- Allegiance to sports

6	Option 1	Male	question 13
28	Option 2		
26	Option 3		
5	Option 1	Female	
9	Option 2		
26	Option 3		

Table 4- Allegiance to sports gender wise

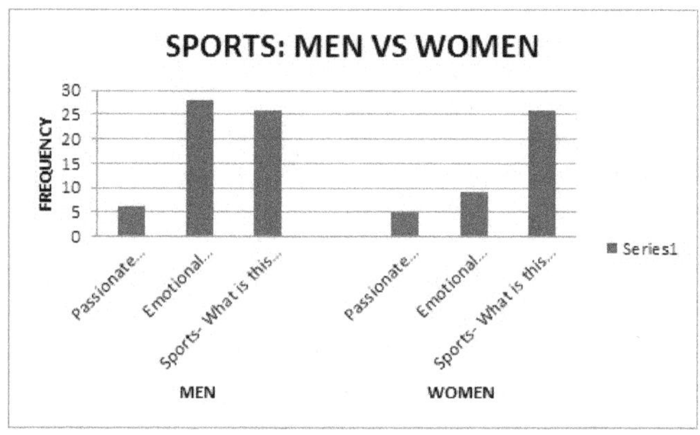

Figure 6- Allegiance to sports gender wise

The data shows that in men, emotional attachment to the allegiance is much greater than in women, who follow the general trend shown in the other "non exception" questions i.e. Option 3>Option2>Option 1.

It may be assumed that male subjects are more passionate about the support they give to sports teams and follow it more religiously. Hence, expressing their support on Facebook is an important part of their psyche. However, option 1, which includes blind following of peers' views, is minimal. This proves a strong independence in opinion from the external influence of peers when it comes to sports.

2) Question 16: Before Course Registration, you ask about a group of teachers (with a prior preference) for a subject on a Facebook platform (VIT Universal Database). You observe the comments. A Facebook friend has commented amidst many others. What would you do?

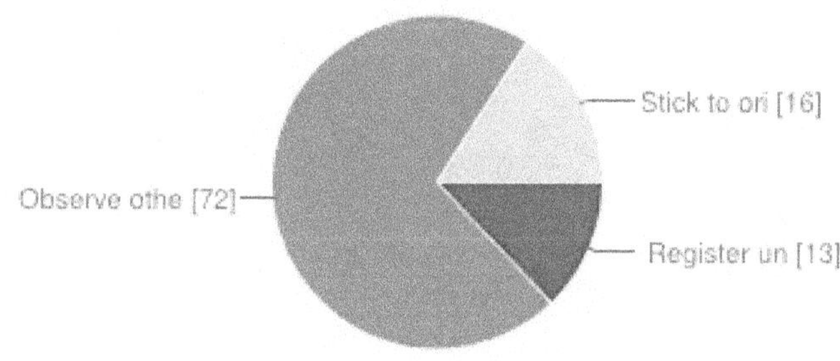

Figure 7- Preferences in course registration

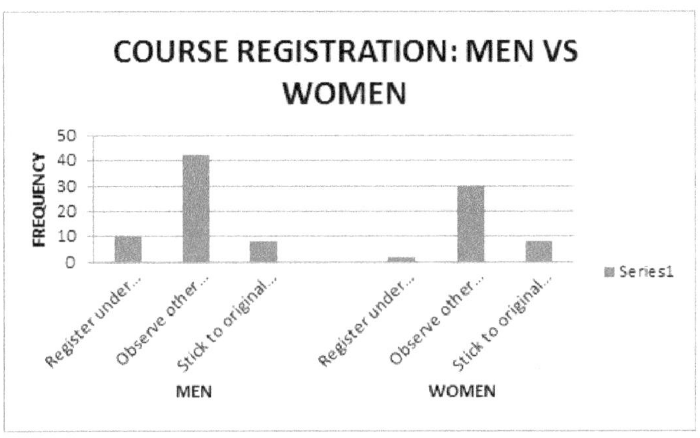

Figure 8- Preferences in course registration gender wise

10	Option 1	male
42	Option 2	
8	Option 3	
2	Option 1	Female
30	Option 2	
8	Option 3	

Table 5- Preferences in course registration gender wise

For both males and females, the VIT populace shows a departure from normal trends. Here Option 2 is highest for both genders. Students would prefer to re-examine their opinion and take the advice of seniors for choosing teachers. Hence, for decisions directly affecting the everyday life of the student, subjects were more hesitant to give blind faith to both their peers (Option1) and themselves (Option 3). They were more circumspect, probably keeping in mind strictness, attendance leniency, marking and so on. They chose to make an informed decision.

3) Question 18-What means of publicity encourages you the most to join a Club/ Chapter on campus?

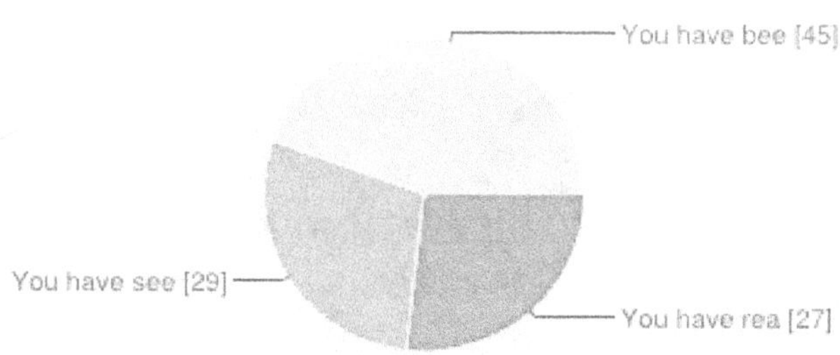

Figure 9- Preferences Club/ Chapter promotion on campus

20	Option 1	Male	Question 18
15	Option 2		
25	Option 3		
6	Option 1	Female	
14	Option 2		
20	Option 3		

Table 6- Preferences Club/ Chapter promotion on campus genderwise

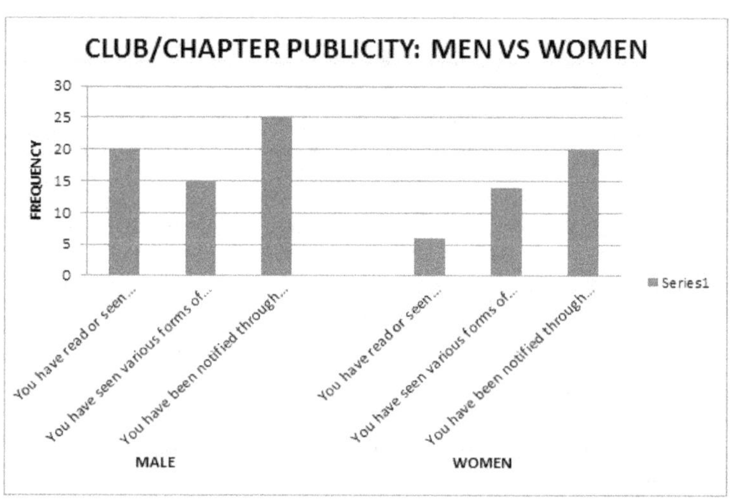

Figure 10- Preferences Club/ Chapter on campus gender wise

Though the overall distribution of subjects as shown in the pie chart follows the popular trend (Option 3>Option2>Option 1), the spread is much more equal as compared to the other "non exception" questions. Option 1 and Option 2 have an almost same frequency, and Option 3 is greatly reduced as compared to other questions. Moreover, (Option 1+Option 2)>Option 3. Thus for joining clubs/chapters, we see a strong collaborative decision-making process. We tend to choose those organisations are friends are a part of. For co-curricular decisions, we tend to stick to our friend group to maximise utility and enjoy ourselves. This trend is greatly pronounced in males over females (they follow the normal trend). It seems males have a stronger tendency to form groups and stick to them, translating virtual friendship to real life friendship. This study shows that males have a greater propensity to form social groups when it comes to matters of recreation and follows their peers.

Conclusion

The null hypothesis is rejected, and Alternate Hypothesis is accepted. A large majority of the subject populace shows a departure from original assumption and is Facebook independent for Lifestyle preferences, Consumer Tastes and Individual Decision making and Opinions. This is contrary to the pre-findings in the papers such as *Identifying Peer Influence in Massive Online Social Networks: A Platform for Randomized Experimentation on Facebook Sinan Aral and Dylan Walker.* They have found out that passive viral messages (notifications, newsfeed items, profile displays) generated a click-through response for new applications. A significant portion (47%) of these click-throughs came from Facebook users who had not previously adopted the application. Of click-throughs by non-application users, 62% resulted in the adoption of the application, indicating a potentially significant response to passive viral messaging. Their initial results demonstrate that the potential for influence is significant in this network. In the sphere of Tastes, *Social selection and peer influence in an online social network by Kevin Lewisa, et al.* states that people start listening to "shared" music by peers on Facebook and other online networking sites. Regarding Consumer Preference, *The Influence of Facebook Friends on Consumers' Purchase Decisions by Alghamdi Mohammed.* The study findings showed that a considerable number of participants usually used Facebook to obtain product recommendations from Facebook friends before they purchased products (about 35%). Approximately 85% of those participants purchased products based on these recommendations. The study found that there was a strong positive correlation between seeking product recommendations from Facebook friends and consumers' purchase decisions based on these recommendations.

However, within our subject group, peer influence does not play such a pivotal role in our decision-making process. The subjects have a strong sense of identity and preserve it despite being exposed to the external peer stimuli online. In fact, they use such a social platform to promote their ideologies, advertise their opinions, receive critical feedback and is supplementing the traditional decision-making cycle with great effect. This is similar to the findings of SNCR's research on Social Media's Impact on Business and Decision Making. Our study shows an absence of blind faith in Facebook friends but a strong need to discuss and come to an informed decision using this modern technology. Facebook does have a profound influence on our personal and public life, but not in the manner we estimated.

References

Alghamdi, M. (2012). The Influence of Facebook Friends on Consumers' Purchase Decisions (Thesis, Master of Science). The University of Otago. Retrieved from http://hdl.handle.net/10523/2164

Aral, S., Walker, D. 2009. *Identifying Peer Influence in Massive Online Social Networks: A Platform for Randomized Experimentation on Facebook.*" Workshop on Information Systems Economics, Phoenix, AZ.

Corbyn, Zoe . (12 September, 2012). Facebook experiment boosts US voter turnout. *Nature Magazine.*

Lewis K, Gonzalez M, Kaufman J. 2012. Social selection and peer influence in an online social network. *Proceedings of the National Academy of Sciences.*109, 68–72.

Society for New Communications Research (SNCR)-Social Media's Impact on Business and Decision Making by Dom Bulmer and Vanessa DiMauro

----

Appendix

Questionnaire

1) Specify your gender. ____________________________________
2) Which School do you belong to? (Mention BRANCH)

____

3) What is the time duration that you spend on Facebook per day?
   a) Less than 1 hour
   b) 1-3 hours
   c) 3-5 hours
   d) More than 5 hours
   e) Depending on my mood.
4) What is the approximate number of Facebook friends you have?
   a) Less than 100
   b) 100-500
   c) 500-1000
   d) 1000-1500
   e) More than 1500
5) How long have you had an active Facebook account?
   a) Less than a year
   b) 1-2 years
   c) 3-5 years

    d) More than 5 years

6) What prompts you to like a Facebook Page?
   a) I was notified because a Facebook friend had LIKED IT/INVITED me
   b) Searched the Page out of my own interest
   c) Page Advertisements on your Facebook Wall.

7) Why would you try a new food?
   a) Because a Facebook friend posted about it
   b) Because you saw an Advertisement/Review on a Sponsored Page on Facebook.
   c) Sources beyond Facebook.

8) How do you hear about new Music?
   a) A Facebook friend had posted/shared about the new artist/genre.
   b) Public accolades/criticism via updates in trending section of Facebook.
   c) Print and Electronic media besides Facebook

9) How do you decide your attire for an occasion (Birthday Party, Marriage, Get Together, etc)?
   a) Facebook discussions with friends over Chats/Group Chats.
   b) Looking up Fashion-centric Facebook Page.
   c) I would choose attire that compliments my personality.

10) What would influence you to purchase a new book?
   a) Update by a Facebook friend on recent books read.
   b) Reader's reviews of the concerned book on Facebook
   c) Professional critique of the book in print and electronic media.

11) How do you choose a brand for your electronic gadgets?
   a) By posting a status or comment asking for recommendations on Facebook.
   b) Updates by the brands themselves about new products on their Facebook page.
   c) Self-Research of specifications of the desired product.

12) How is your brand consciousness of clothes influenced?
   a) Pictures uploaded with references to a particular clothing line in status by a friend on Facebook.
   b) Preference is determined by public figures or celebrities on Facebook.
   c) I just want clothes- No brand preference.

13) How do you decide your Sports Allegiances (Individuals, Clubs or Nations)?
   a) Passionate declarations made by your Facebook friends concerning that particular sport.
   b) Emotional attachment to what the allegiance represents which includes public support on Facebook.
   c) Sports- What is this you talk about?-No such allegiance exists.

14) I am a fan/hater of a specific Soap/Serial because-
   a) My Facebook friends gave a glowing/bitter review of it.
   b) Various public platforms on Facebook endorsed its fandom/boredom
   c) I don't watch such shows/ My connection with the show is independent of Facebook

15) Why would you put up a status on a Current Affair (e.g., 2014 General Elections)?
a) Your Facebook friend group has been posting about it recently, and you wish to seem knowledgeable/fit in.
b) You want to initiate a logical discussion on the topic with your peers using Facebook as a platform.
c) You genuinely believe in the opinion you have posted and have preconceived

notions about it.

16) Before Course Registration, you ask about a group of teachers (with a prior preference) for a subject on a Facebook platform (VIT Universal Database). You observe the comments. A Facebook friend has commented amidst many others. What would you do?

    a) Register under the teacher your Facebook friend suggested.

    b) Observe other comments and verify with seniors via chat/messages.

    c) Stick to original choice, irrespective of any comments.

17) During Course Registration you see Facebook friends put up their Time Table. You would-

    a) Model your Time Table according to theirs.

    b) You will wait for further analysis by others on various aspects of the Time Table.

    c) Go with your own decision based on your preferences(Morning/Afternoon, Attendance and so on).

18) What means of publicity encourages you the most to join a Club/ Chapter on campus?

    a) You have read or seen accounts, experiences, pictures or "shares" of a particular Club/Chapter by a Facebook friend.

    b) You have seen various forms of publicity of the Club/Chapter on Facebook by the organisation itself. (Note: Not individual members but the official club page itself)

    c) You have been notified through on-campus publicity.

19) For the General Elections of 2014 has your opinion on whom to vote for being molded most by

    a) Ideals espoused by Facebook friends in the form of statuses, videos, articles shared by them.

    b) General ridicule/ promotion of candidates on public platforms on Facebook by now Facebook friends.

    c) Genuine interest in the manifesto and policies of those candidates eligible for election.

20) There are social movements occurring in the nation. (Anti-rape, Female foeticide and so on). Your views, awareness, and participation in the real world vis-a-vis these movements is most affected by-

    a) Posts made Facebook friends about the movement supporting/belittling it.

    b) Public declarations by personalities or updates by well-known public pages on Facebook.

    c) Discussion, research, and deliberation about the movement.

Chapter 3

Effects of Facebook on Social Relationships

Vineet Mohan & Shubham Jha

Introduction

Facebook was founded in 2004 by Mark Zuckerberg and his college roommates. It was originally designed for Harvard students only. It gradually expanded to Ivy League colleges and Stanford University, and today is open to all users around the world over the age of 13. According to the Wall Street Journal, as of September 2012, Facebook has one billion active users of which 9% are fake accounts.

Facebook is a social networking website, aimed at connecting people worldwide with their friends and family. It also allows its users to expand their friend circle and meet new people. Users can create their profiles, add photos, comment, and post on other users' profiles and photos and 'like' them, among several other activities. The activities of users often affect other users who can result in complications and misunderstandings. Articles from TIME Magazine and CNN.com say that Facebook is used as an" interpersonal electronic surveillance" which can create jealousy. "Over 60% of college students use Facebook to check up on their significant others." Facebook has caused "Digital Intimacy", in which studies have shown that 3/5 men and 4/5 women sleep together sooner than they normally would. Facebook is the #1 social networking website used as a tool to find evidence of infidelity in divorce cases and can even be a cause of infidelity. The Facebook "relationship status" has affected our culture's definitions of relationships. By using Facebook, when a relationship will start, and end may be determined by examining friend relationships and communication patterns. Creator of Facebook, Mark Zuckerberg, can determine with 33% accuracy who a user was going to be in a relationship with a week from now. To deduce this, he studied who was looking at which profiles, who your friends were friends with, and who was newly single, among other indicators."

The purpose of this study is to analyze the influence of Facebook on social, interpersonal relationships of students in VIT University, Vellore, India. VIT consists of several thousand students, many of whom are avid Facebook users. This provides a relatively large sample size for the study. VIT students are in the age group of the majority of Facebook users and thus can offer us a more accurate picture. The primary goal is to study changes in interpersonal behaviour between friends, strangers, groups, and partners.

Methodology

Data Collection

This descriptive study was conducted using a survey method. The population comprised of students from VIT University, Vellore. A questionnaire was created, and a survey was taken online with help from docs.google.com at the following link:

https://docs.google.com/forms/d/1vXBseYsii7LJWhiwHR2hgjWiWSoCc8MRx3-uqdl0Tnc/viewform

The questionnaire was answered by random VIT University students. The responses selected were limited to 20 students from various backgrounds.

Data Analysis Techniques

The questions were framed, and feedbacks were received in Microsoft Excel. A descriptive analysis of the data collected was also done in Microsoft Excel.

Results and Discussion

The following were the results obtained from the various responses:

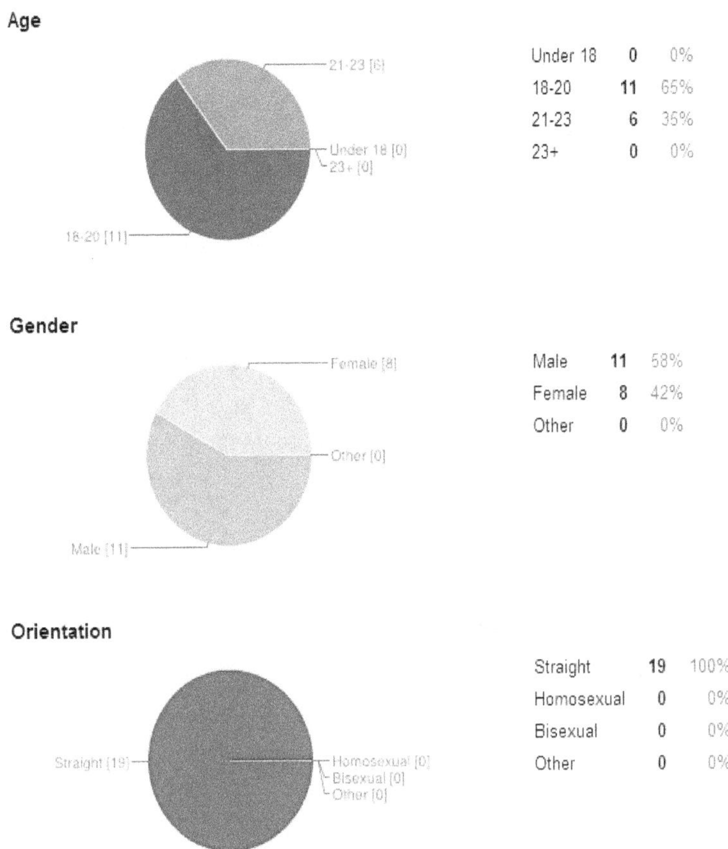

Figure 1- Influence of Facebook on social, interpersonal relationships (age, gender, orientation wise)

As can be seen from the above-given pie charts, 65% of the students who took the survey were in the 18-20 age group, and the remaining 35% were in the 21-23 age group. 58% were male, 42% were female, and all of them admitted to being straight in their orientation. This formed the basis of the personal information that was submitted. The next step was to look into whether or not they owned a Facebook account.

79% of all students had active Facebook accounts, although their frequency of use would require further investigation. 15% of students had deactivated their Facebook accounts, and only 5% of students did not have Facebook accounts. This would indicate that Facebook has become an integral part of the student lifestyle.

When we investigated the frequency of use (Figure 2), it was found that 67% of users browsed Facebook at least once a day although only 22% of users would make posts or comments on that same day.

The standard reason for creating a Facebook account seems universal, i.e., to keep in touch with close friends and those from old schools and colleges. However, a 2% minority exists that joined Facebook just to play games.

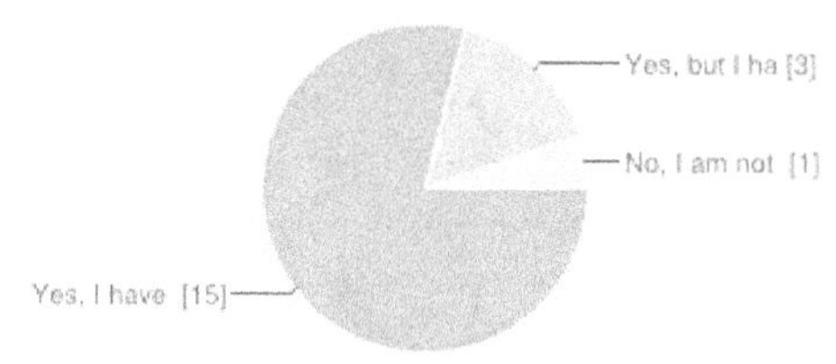

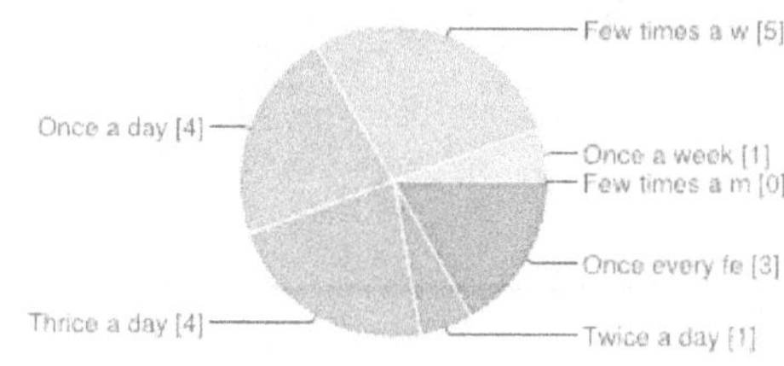

How often do you browse through Facebook?		
Once every few hours	3	17%
Twice a day	1	6%
Thrice a day	4	22%
Once a day	4	22%
Few times a week	5	28%
Once a week	1	6%
Few times a month	0	0%

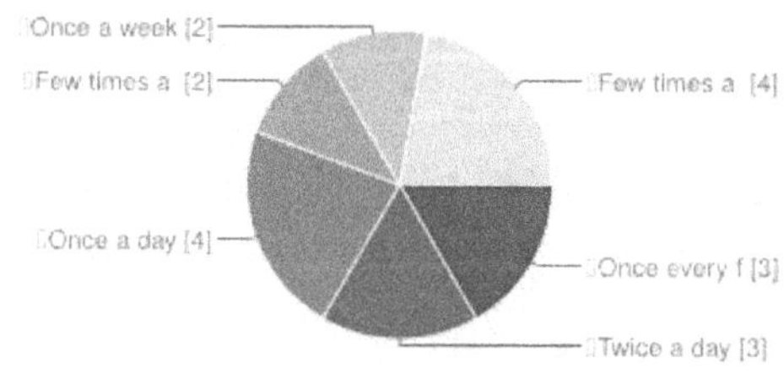

How often are you active on Facebook		
☐Once every few hours	3	17%
☐Twice a day	3	17%
☐Once a day	4	22%
☐Few times a week	2	11%
☐Once a week	2	11%
☐Few times a month	4	22%

Figure 2- Frequency of activity on Facebook

56% of users were not in any relationships, and 28% of them were in committed relationships (Figure 3). However, only 17% registered their status as 'in a committed relationship' on Facebook. 28% of users prefer to keep their relationship status a secret - be it single or committed.

Only 50% of those in a relationship tag their partners in their relationship and those that do often place some value on the status. To them it becomes a statement; it is necessary that people know who they are involved with.

A person's relationship status on Facebook is the key to social relationships. 24% of users have admitted to keeping their status hidden, irrespective of being in a relationship or not because they like to keep the option of having a new relationship open. This aspect allows Facebook users to engage in new relationships and meet new people.

In fact, the opinion that those people who have a hidden relationship status are single is widely disputed. 50% of users believe that they are not single while 44% say that most of them are.

As far as meeting new people and forming new relationships goes, 44% of users have admitted that they would not mind going on a date with someone they met on Facebook.

Facebook, being a social tool is bound to cause problems as well. 53% of users have had problems with their partners/friends due to activities on Facebook. 44% of users have also made posts on impulse to make themselves feel better, which have often led to more harm in the relationship.

What is your relationship status in real life?

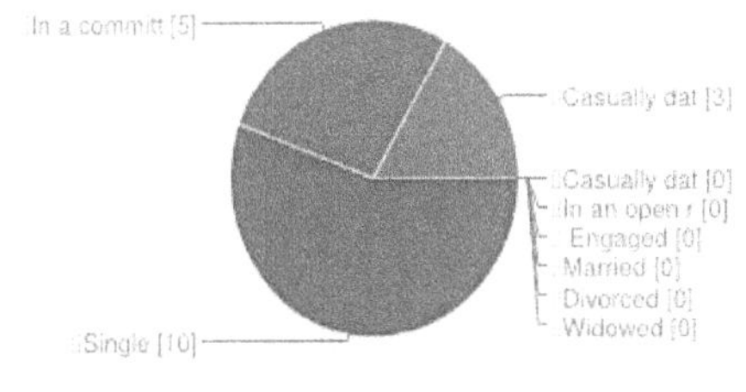

⊐Single	10	56%
⊐In a committed relationship	5	28%
⊐Casually dating a single person	3	17%
⊐Casually dating multiple people	0	0%
⊐In an open relationship	0	0%
⊐ Engaged	0	0%
⊐Married	0	0%
⊐Divorced	0	0%
⊐Widowed	0	0%

What is your status on Facebook?

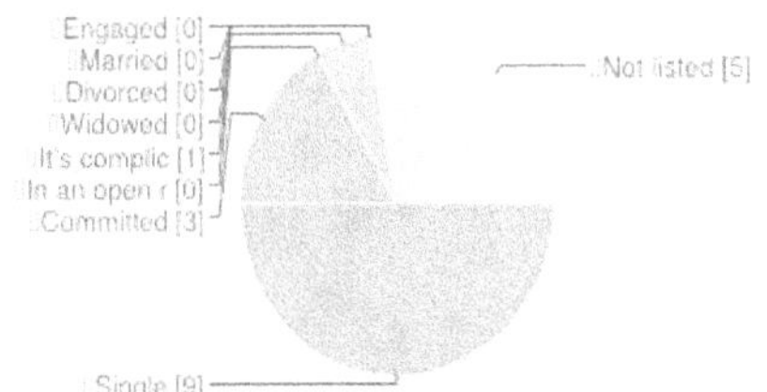

⊐Single	9	50%
⊐Committed	3	17%
⊐In an open relationship	0	0%
⊐It's complicated	1	6%
⊐Engaged	0	0%
⊐Married	0	0%
⊐Divorced	0	0%
⊐Widowed	0	0%
⊐Not listed	5	28%

Do you think all people who have not listed their relationship status on Facebook are single?

Yes, all of them	1	6%
Yes, most of them	8	44%
No	9	50%

Figure 3- Influence of Facebook on social, interpersonal relationships (relationship stats wise)

Have you ever had problems with your friends/significant others due to Facebook?

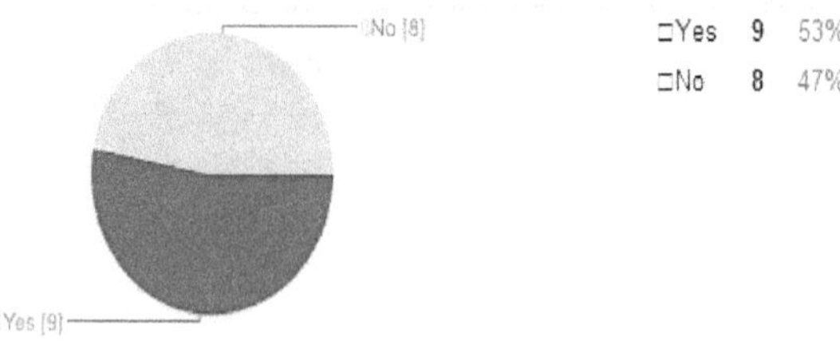

Yes	9	53%
No	8	47%

Have you ever posted on your friend's/significant other's wall to make a point/to relax your jealous instincts?

Yes	8	44%
No	10	56%

Have you ever considered deleting your Facebook?

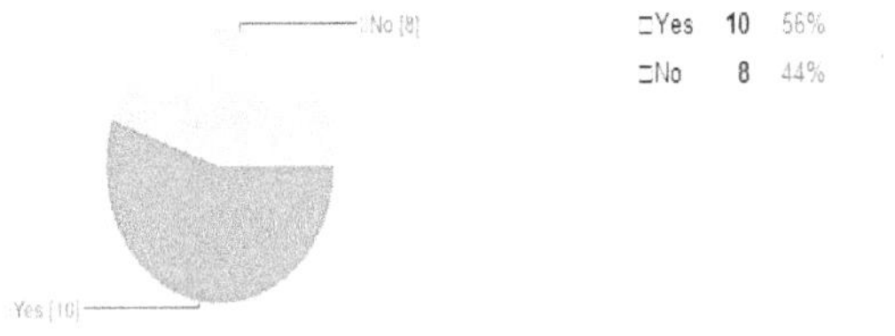

Have you felt distracted from your goals/priorities in the past while using Facebook?

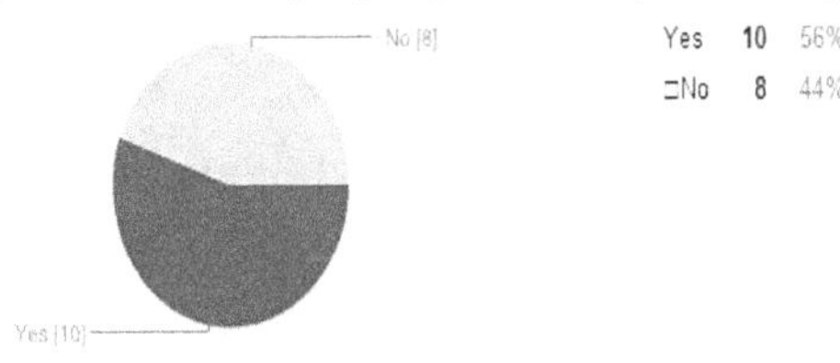

Do you think Facebook has changed your life?

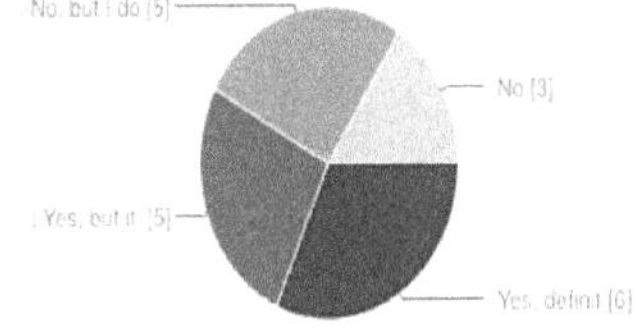

Figure 4- Facebook and perception towards life

55% of users have admitted to thinking about deleting their Facebook accounts (Figure 4) as they feel the social networking site has distracted them from achieving their primary goals. As the sample population is a student base, this particular statistic isn't very surprising.

In the end, however, Facebook still fulfills its primary objective of keeping people in touch and aiding in communication with 84% of users admitting it can change lives, of which 32% can confirm that it has changed their lives for the better.

Conclusion

Post analysis we have determined that Facebook is an integral part of student lifestyle and a huge portion of the student population uses the website on a daily basis. Facebook has encouraged users to be more open about their relationships but at the same time promotes privacy. However, due to the openness of content, an individual who hides his or her details will appear suspicious and can cause curiosity and even distress in a relationship that the said individual may have. Facebook can cause misunderstandings in relationships and even lead to some rash, impulsive actions. These actions can make or break relationships. Ultimately the effect that Facebook has on a relationship is determined by the level of privacy or openness that the two individuals are willing to share.

References

Roy, J. (2013). The Effects of Facebook on Interpersonal Relationships: Blog for MCO345 class at Arizona State University.

Chapter 4

Effects of Facebook on Academic Performance

Stuti Mehrotra, Sakshi Dubey, & Sharon Tess Joy

Introduction

Facebook is a social networking website which allows anyone who claims to be at least 13 years old to become its registered user. Users must register before using the site, after which they may create a personal profile, add other users as friends, exchange messages, and receive automatic notifications when they update their profile. Facebook has over one billion active users of which approximately 9% are fake. Mark Zuckerberg, the founder of Facebook, always said, "Facebook was started not just to be a company, but to fulfill a vision of connecting the world".

The present study aims to analyse the influence of Facebook on the academic performance of students in VIT University, Vellore, India. Each student spends a certain no. of hours per day on an average, as per his/her wish. The study seeks a relationship between the duration of time spent on Facebook and the academic performance (based on CGPA).

Factor Affecting Academics Performance

A number of studies (Diaz, 2003; Crosnoe, Johnson, and Elder, 2004) have been carried out to identify the various factors influencing the academic performance of students in some institutions worldwide. Theory of Educational Productivity by Walberg (1981) determined three groups of nine elements based on affective, cognitive and behavioral skills for optimization of learning that affect the quality of academic performance: aptitude (ability, development and motivation); instruction (amount and quality); environment (home, classroom, peers and television) (Roberts, 2007). On the other hand, Mushtaq and Khan (2012) suggest that two types of factors that affect the students' academic performance are internal and external classroom factors. Internal classroom factors include students' competence in English, class schedules, class size, English textbooks, class test results, learning facilities, homework, the environment of the class, the complexity of the course material, teachers' role in the class, the technology used in the class and exams systems. External classroom factors include extracurricular activities, family problems, work and financial, social and other problems. However, Mlambo (2011) argues that the combination of factors influencing academic performance varies from one educational environment to another, from one set of students to the next, and indeed from one cultural setting to another. Therefore, the present study aims to investigate the influence of Facebook as a factor in academic performance.

Methodology

Sampling and Data Collection

This descriptive study was conducted using a survey method. The population comprised of students from VIT University, Vellore. A questionnaire was created, and a survey was taken online with help from docs.google.com at the following link:

https://docs.google.com/forms/d/1c5KfdVhSayOELI4uZ6A508viY1EYn4I2c7pceU-9L3Q/viewform

The questionnaire was answered by random VIT University students. The responses selected were limited to 159 students who were from different departments/courses of study. The study was limited only to the various salient features of Facebook.

Data Analysis Techniques

The questions were framed, and feedbacks were received in Microsoft Excel. A descriptive analysis of the data collected was also done in Microsoft Excel.

Results and Discussion

We conducted this survey in VIT University to study the impact of Facebook on the academic performance of the students. 159 students took this online survey, the summary of which is presented below. 67% of the participants were males. 60% of the participants had their CGPAs in the range of 8.1 to 9.0.

Majority of the Facebook users are among the age group 18-22. And most of the students who spend a lot of time on Facebook are between the age group of 16-20. Around 38% of the people use Facebook more than three times a day. Most of the students who took this survey had 200-400 friends on their friend list. 54% of the people confessed to using Facebook during classroom hours occasionally. 36% of the students tend to use Facebook once in 2-3 hours while studying. A whopping 65% have never used Facebook to communicate with their professors. 53% of these people agreed that Facebook negatively affects the quality of their work. 50% of the students believe that Facebook is a useful learning tool. 59% of Facebook users denied that Facebook hadn't had any impact at all on their CGPA. However, 40% believe that Facebook might have impacted their CGPA in a somewhat, negative manner.

Conclusion

There are various factors inside and outside the college that contribute to the quality of academic performance of students. The present study only focused on the students' attitude towards the different aspects of Facebook and the influence it has on the students' academic achievement as represented by their CGPA. It is clear from the results that the Facebook is both good and bad for the students in VIT University, as the students with higher CGPA are more satisfied with its role in providing a medium for interaction on study-related topics. However, there is a level of dissatisfaction as well. It will be beneficial if students do not overspend their time on Facebook, and use it judiciously.

References

Facebook and Academic Performance. (n.d.). Retrieved January 11, 2018, from https://www.surveymonkey.com/s/VRGQJ8R

Ogedebe, P. M., Emmanuel, J. A., & Musa, Y. (n.d.). A survey on Facebook and Academic Performance in Nigeria Universities. Retrieved January 11, 2018, from http://www.ijera.com/pages/v2no4.html

Rouis, S., Limayem, M., & Salehi-Sangari, E. (2016, September 29). Impact of Facebook usage on students' academic achievement: the role of self-regulation and trust. Retrieved January 11, 2018, from http://pure.ltu.se/portal/en/publications/impact-of-Facebook-usage-on-students-academic-achievement(da225aa0-0025-402f-a145-05e6fb0c7e20).html

Chapter 5

Influence of Facebook on Obsessive Compulsive Disorder (OCD)

Poulomi Adhikari, Mekhla Singhania, & Pearl Moharil

Introduction

OCD (Obsessive Compulsive Disorders)

Obsessive-compulsive disorder (OCD) is an anxiety disorder characterized by intrusive thoughts that produce uneasiness, apprehension, fear, or worry; by repetitive behaviors aimed at reducing the associated anxiety; or by a combination of such obsessions and compulsions. People with obsessive-compulsive disorders find their obsessions or compulsive distressing and devitalizing but feel unable to stop them. The anxiety and tension associated with obsessions- persistent unwanted thoughts, impulses, or ideas- or compulsions- results in seemingly irrational behaviour repeatedly carried out in a fixed, repetitive way.

With OCD, you may or may not realize that your obsessions aren't reasonable, and you may try to ignore them or stop them. But that only increases your distress and anxiety. Ultimately, you feel driven to perform compulsive acts to ease your stressful feelings.

Obsessive-compulsive disorder affects children and adolescents, as well as adults. Roughly one third to one-half of adults with OCD report a childhood onset of the disorder, suggesting the continuum of anxiety disorders across the lifespan. Obsessive-compulsive disorder symptoms usually include both obsessions and compulsions. But it's also possible to have only obsession symptoms or only compulsion symptoms.

 OCD often centers on themes, such as a fear of getting contaminated by germs. To ease your contamination fears, you may compulsively wash your hands until they're sore and chapped. Despite efforts to ignore these thoughts, they keep coming back. This leads to more ritualistic behavior — and a vicious cycle that's characteristic of OCD.

Examples of obsession signs and symptoms include fear of being contaminated by shaking hands or by touching objects others have touched, doubts that you've locked the door or turned off the stove, intense stress when objects aren't orderly or facing a certain way, etc.

As with obsessions, compulsions typically have themes, such as washing and cleaning, counting, checking, demanding reassurances, following a strict routine and orderliness Examples of compulsion signs and symptoms include hand-washing until your skin becomes raw, checking doors repeatedly to make sure they're locked, checking the stove repeatedly to make sure it's off, etc.

Despite the irrational behaviour, OCD is sometimes associated with above-average intelligence. Its sufferers commonly share personality traits such as high attention to detail, avoidance of risk, careful planning, exaggerated sense of responsibility and a tendency to take time in making decisions. Multiple psychological and biological factors may be involved in causing obsessive-compulsive syndromes. OCD has been linked to abnormalities with the neurotransmitter serotonin, although it could be either a cause or an effect of these abnormalities. Researchers have yet to pinpoint the exact cause of OCD, but brain differences, genetic influences, and environmental factors are being studied.

The relation between OCD and Facebook

The Canadian Herbert Marshall McLuhan once said the world had become a global village through technology, and indeed it is here with us today. In our time, just at the click of a bottom, a person can communicate with anybody at any corner in the world. Communication has to do with verbal or non-verbal mediums which are transmitted through the message. The social networking sites that have brought millions together around the world could be generating obsessive-compulsive disorder (OCD) among its users. The most famous social networking site 'Facebook' has got millions of users. Facebook was founded on February 4, 2004, by Mark Zuckerberg with his college roommates and fellow Harvard University students Eduardo Saverin, Andrew McCollum, Dustin MoskoVITz and Chris Hughes. The founders had initially limited the website's membership to Harvard students but later expanded it to colleges in the Boston area, the Ivy League, and Stanford University. It gradually added support for students at various other universities before it opened to high-school students, and eventually to anyone aged 13 and over. Facebook now allows anyone who claims to be at least 13 years old to become a registered user of the website.

Many psychological disorders have arisen due to excessive use of social networking sites like Facebook. One such malady is Obsessive-Compulsive Facebook Disorder (OCFD). This happens when you are so addicted to Facebook that you keep going to your Facebook account although at that moment it doesn't seem to be a necessity. So, in the end, you scroll up and down and keep on reading your friends' updates and posts. It is like a constant obsession to go to to your Facebook homepage now and then even if there are no new notifications, just to get a feeling of satisfaction. You may be in the middle of a meeting or dialogue, but you brood about who might be online to chat with you. The obsessive thoughts may often be linked with compulsive acts. At times, the persistent thought of losing a social networking friend or the feeling of attending to some online friends recurring urges one to perform ritualistic behaviours. But when a person has an obsessive-compulsive disorder, such thoughts and urges, occupy so much time that they seriously interfere with daily life. Many might be aware of this problem but will not know where and who to turn to, while others may not have come to the realization that what they are battling with is this disorder.

Nielsen Online reports that social networking (and associated blogging) is now the fourth most popular online actiVITy, ahead of personal e-mail and behind only search engines. It also reports that the 70 million Facebook members in the U.S. spent 233 million hours on the site in April 2009, up from 28 million hours by 23 million members the previous April—a 175 percent increase in per capita usage. Also according to a study by Nucleus Research in Boston, the most avid users are spending two hours a day on the site while they are at work—helping to cost companies whose employees can access Facebook 1.5 percent of total office productivity.

A study conducted by Craig Ross, Emily Orr, Mia Sisic, Jamie Arseneault, Mary Simmering and Robert Orr presented the idea that identity presentation influences the use of Facebook. Portions of the NEO personality inventory were drawn from the original 181-factor analysis to distinguish personality traits of respondents. They tested the extent to which certain situational factors such as boredom and procrastination could affect an individual's usage of Facebook, therefore considering them a Facebook addict. The dependent variable in this study was the amount to which an individual is addicted to Facebook.

Addictions to the Internet have been examined in previous literature with varieties of other independent variables such as behavior type, behavior type, types of Internet usage and so forth. Previous literature on addiction to social media has been conducted on the basis of Griffiths' Six Criteria (Cabral 9), but there was no work done to test Facebook in particular. This study was focused on conducting data associated directly with Facebook and the usage thereof. Conclusions were drawn from the respondents to prove if they are or are not addicted to Facebook and these conclusions were tested to find correlations between behavior types and the types of internet usages acting as a facilitator for Facebook addiction. Respondents were questioned on the basis of usage of Facebook, the feelings they have when they use Facebook, and the amount to which they feel connected to Facebook in a way that feels impossible to let go of.

The study was conducted on 77 undergraduate students at the University of Massachusetts- Boston, College Of Management. However, despite an extraverts desire to socialize and continuously connect with individuals, they are not more likely to be addicted to Facebook

Further, it was predicted that females are more likely to be addicted to Facebook than their male counterparts.

A study conducted by Szczegielniak, A., Pakła, K. and Krysta, K., the impact of social networking on the ongoing behavior of respondents was assessed. It was the first step of a study on the possibility of dependence on social networks. The study was based on an authors' questionnaire placed on popular polish websites in February 2013. Questions related to the types and frequency of specific activities undertaken by the private profiles of users. The study involved 221 respondents, 193 questionnaires were filled in completely and correctly, without missing any questions. 83.24% admitted to using social networking sites, 16.76% indicated that they never had their profile. An overwhelming number of respondents is a member of Facebook (79.17%), specialized portals related to their profession or work were used by only 13.89%, Our-class (6.25%) and Twitter was a primary portal for one person only. Hence the conclusion was that there is a big difference between the addiction to the Internet and addictions existing within the Internet; the same pattern applies to social networking. There is a need to recognize the "social networking" for a particular activity, irrespective of Facebook, Twitter, and Nasza-Klasa, which are commercial products.

David Disalvo, a science, technology, and culture writer based in Florida, mentioned in his article "Are social networks messing with your head?", that most people will not imperil their psyches if they spend a little more time on social-networking sites. For them, two hours a day on Facebook may simply mean two hours less in front of the TV. But for people who bring a compulsive personality to the keyboard, those hours can grow rapidly, setting off a cascade of bad consequences at home and work. "Someone with obsessive-compulsive tendencies is predisposed to a range of addictive behaviors," says neuroscientist Gary Small of the University of California, Los Angeles, He also says, "Technology has a way of accelerating the compulsive process."

Social media researcher Scott Caplan of the University of Delaware says, "People who prefer online interaction over face-to-face interaction also score higher on measures of compulsive Internet use and using the Internet to alter their moods". In 2007 Caplan conducted a study of 343 undergraduate students to determine what stoked the fires of compulsive behavior online. He homed in on personality traits that leave people vulnerable, such as loneliness and social anxiety, and online actiVITies that attract people with compulsive tendencies, such as playing video games, watching pornography and gambling.

Of these variables, social anxiety emerged as the strongest. "Socially anxious individuals who have problems with face-to-face interactions are drawn to the unique features of online conversation," Caplan says. In time, they may start using social networking compulsively to regulate their mood, and the self-feeding cycle begins.

All the articles that have been mentioned above relate to different communities. A different community may have a different response to the same parameters. So the results for different communities may change. Hence we aim to survey VIT University community. So our targets are the students of VIT, and we aim to find signs of obsession with Facebook among our target audience.

Literature Review

In the article "Links Among Obsessive-Compulsive Personality Characteristics and Facebook Usage" written by Authors Stevens, Sarah; Humphrey, Karissa; Wheatley, TaLisha, Galliher, Renee.V, Facebook users were invited as participants to complete a survey about Facebook use and personality characteristics. The survey included the Leyton Obsessional Inventory, and a Facebook questionnaire was posted online through a survey tool, Psychdata. There was no relation found among the frequency or time spent on Facebook and obsessive-compulsive personality characteristics, but significant relations were found among reasons for accessing Facebook and obsessive-compulsive personality characteristics. These findings suggest that individuals with obsessive-compulsive personality characteristics may engage in Facebook as a way to ease stress.

In the "Facebook OCD causes depression" written by Shea Morgan on March 14, 2013, discussions about the growing trend of depression amongst teenagers were conducted. Teen depression.org reported that nearly 20 percent of teens struggle with depression before reaching adulthood. This problem, affecting one in five young people, is becoming a big issue, and some researchers are pointing to social networking as a major cause. Since there is a sense of pleasure when a Facebook post is "liked" or commented on, the user can grow much attached to checking and re-checking his/her account. This severe phenomenon, known as Facebook OCD, can become an intense habit and can even be addictive. It also reports that social networks have become a prime place for bullying. It is much easier and takes far less courage to type someone a hurtful message rather than confronting him or her in person. For this reason, it has become common to use the Internet as a tool for bullying. It also shows that Facebook OCD affects the social life.

The article "Applying the uses and gratifications theory to exploring friend-networking sites" by Raacke, J., and Bonds-Raacke, J. shows that the increased use of the Internet is a new tool in communication has changed the way people interact. This fact is even more evident in the recent development and use of friend-networking sites. Therefore, this study was conducted to evaluate: (a) why people use these friend-networking sites, (b) what the characteristics are of the typical college user, and (c) what uses and gratifications are met by using these sites. Results indicated that the vast majority of college students are using these friend-networking sites for a significant portion of their day for reasons such as making new friends and locating old friends. It was also found that men and women of traditional college age and all ethnic groups are equally engaging in this form of online communication.

In the article: "The benefits of Facebook "friends:" Social capital and college students' use of online social network sites" by Ellison, N.B., Steinfield, C., Lampe, C. A study was conducted to examine the relationship between use of Facebook, and the formation and maintenance of social capital. Social capital assesses one's ability to stay connected with members of a previously inhabited community. Analyses conducted on results from a survey of about 286 undergraduate students suggest a strong association between use of Facebook and the three types of social capital, with the strongest relationship being to bridging social capital. Also, Facebook usage was found to interact with measures of psychological well-being, suggesting that it might provide greater benefits for users experiencing low self-esteem and low life satisfaction.

In an article "Social network's effects on Italian teenager's life" by Guzzo, T., Ferri, F., Grifoni, P.(Institute of Research on Population and Social Policies, National Research Council of Italy, Italy). A survey was conducted to gather data collected using an online questionnaire filled in by 414 teenagers. The statistics indicated that the use of social networks seems to have a positive impact on sociality of the teenagers involved in the survey. In fact, according to information provided by them, the use of social networks mainly aims to improve face-to-face relationships. However, some of them use it as a showcase creating idealized profiles to be accepted from the group, increasing in some cases online friendships and reducing that face-to-face

Many articles showed that Facebook had a severe effect on the academics of students. In an article "Facebook and academic performance" by Kirschner, P.A., Karpinski, A.C, it was said that there is much talk of a change in modern youth-often referred to as digital natives or Homo Zappiens-with respect to their ability to simultaneously process multiple channels of information. In other words, kids today can multitask. However, statistics show that such behavior leads to both increased study time to achieve learning parity and an increase in mistakes while processing information than those who are sequentially or serially processing that same information. This article presents the results of a descriptive and exploratory survey study involving the Facebook use, often carried out simultaneously with other study activities, and its relation to academic performance as measured by self-reported Grade Point Average (GPA) and hours spent studying per week. Results show that Facebook users reported having lower GPAs and spend fewer hours per week studying than nonusers.

But in another article of the same topic, by Pasek, J., More, E., Hargittai, E. It stated that the above results were based on correlational data in a draft manuscript that had not been published. In none of the samples did they find a robust negative relationship between Facebook use and grades. Indeed, if anything, Facebook use is more common among individuals with higher grades. It also examined how changes in academic performance in the nationally representative sample related to Facebook use and found that Facebook users were no different from non-users.

In an article "Online social networking and addiction-A review of the psychological literature" by Kuss, D.J. , Griffiths, M.D. the emerging phenomenon of addiction to SNSs (Social Networking Sites) was studied by: (1) outlining SNS usage patterns, (2) examining motivations for SNS usage, (3) examining personalities of SNS users, (4) examining negative consequences of SNS usage, (5) exploring potential SNS addiction, and (6) exploring SNS addiction specificity and comorbidity. The result stated that the extraverts appear to use social networking sites for social enhancement, whereas introverts use it for social compensation, each of which appears to be related to greater usage, as does low conscientiousness and high narcissism. Negative correlates of SNS usage include the decrease in real life social community participation and academic achievement, as well as relationship problems, each of which may be indicative of potential addiction.

A similar study was done in the article 'Analysis of the psychological traits, Facebook usage, and Facebook addiction model of Taiwanese university students 'by Hong, F.-Y. , Huang, D.-H. , Lin, H.-Y. , Chiu, S.-L. The purposes of the study were to (1) identify the role of the psychological traits of university students in Facebook addiction and Facebook usage, and (2) explore the correlation between Facebook usage and Facebook addiction. This study treated 241 university students in Taiwan as the research subjects, and adopted the Rosenberg's self-esteem scale, Lai's personality test, a Facebook usage scale, and a Facebook addiction scale (FAS). The structured equation modeling (SEM) was used for data analysis. The results showed that: (1) self-inferiority could significantly predict Facebook usage; and (2) having a depressive character and Facebook usage can significantly predict Facebook addiction.

In the article: "Malaysian Facebookers: Motives and addictive behaviours unraveled" by Balakrishnan, V, Shamim, A., Malaysians were reported to have the most number of Facebook friends, spend more time on Facebook and might be addicted to Facebook as well. Results show that Malaysian students use Facebook actively, similar to other studies done worldwide. Factor analyses yielded five motives to use Facebook: Social Networking, Psychological Benefits, Entertainment, Self-Presentation and Skill Enhancement. As for the behavioural symptoms, Salience, Loss of Control, Withdrawal and Relapse and Reinstatement emerged as the four main symptoms.

A similar article on:" Addictive Facebook use among university students" by Zaremohzzabieh, Z., Samah, B.A., Omar, S.Z., Bolong, J., Akhtar, N., Kamarudin, N.A. indicated that this social networking site could become addictive to some university students' users. The aim of this study, therefore, is to explore the phenomenon of Facebook addiction among university students. The study using interview was used to gather data from nine International postgraduates of Universiti Putra Malaysia, and the data established three themes - Compulsion to check Facebook, High-frequency use, and Using Facebook to avoid offline responsibility. The findings from these three themes showed that these users considered their Facebook dependency, are known as salience, tolerance, and conflict. These results also lead to the conclusion that like most actiVITies, moderation and controlled use are key. So, the best approach to preparing students for life in a knowledge-based society is to help them exercise self-control and achieve a level of balance when using Facebook.

In another article on "Effect of Facebook on the life of Medical University students" by Farooqi, H. , Patel, H. , Aslam, H.M. , Ansari, I.Q. , Khan, M. , Iqbal, N. , Rasheed, H. , Jabbar, Q. , Khan, S.R. , Khalid, B. , Nadeem, A. , Afroz, R., Shafiq, S., Mustafa, A , Asad, N. saw a cross sectional, observational and questionnaire based study was conducted in Dow University OF Health Sciences during the period of January 2012 to November 2012. The results were as follows: Out of total 1000 participants, 40% were males, and 60% were females. Participants were in the age group of 18-25 years with a mean age of 20.08 years. Most of the participants were using Facebook daily (64%) for around 3-4 hours (40.1%). Majority of them (35.9%) believed that they were equally active on Facebook and in real life while few believed their social life became worse after start using Facebook (37.2%). Most of the participants admitted that they were considered as shy in the real world (39.0%) while in the world of Facebook they were considered as fun loving by their friends (60.3%). A large number of participants (75%) complained of mood swings.

Thus, it was concluded that youngsters are willing to compromise their health, social life, studies for the sake of fun and entertainment or whatever satisfaction they get from using Facebook. Our observance concluded that majority of the users are highly addicted.

Methodology

In our survey, our target group was the students and faculty of VIT University. We got a total of 163 responses out of which 44% were from the age bracket of 13-18,52% from 19- 25 and the remaining from above 25. Out of our target group, 90% have a smartphone. Out of that only 3 people (2%) use Facebook more than four hours a day. A total of 144 students (89%) have been using Facebook for 3 or more years. The majority (42%) have Facebook friends in the range of 501 to 1000. So the factor of sociability is high.

Results and Discussion

Most people do not start their day by logging in to Facebook (78%), and also only a few people admit to regularly updating their Facebook statuses (88%). So the urge to log in to Facebook is low.

Showing extreme signs of obsession, 44% people admitted to using Facebook as the first thing when they open their laptops. A large percentage (71%) use Facebook late at night.

In fact, only 12% fantasize about making their next great Facebook update. The majority (96%) people declined Facebook to be the only mode of communication between them and their family. Though 2% people admitted to enrolling in photography courses for the sake of Facebook pictures, 2% people have resorted to paying off strangers to become their friends.4% People admitted that their relationship affects their Facebook status. Also, 21% admit to meeting virtual friends. Hence there is a relationship between real life and virtual life.

A very small percentage(18%) do get angry if pictures of any special outing are not uploaded and tagged. 20% do admit to feeling depressed due to negative comments on them. So their sense of pleasure/ displeasure does get affected by posts and comments.

72% do admit to scrolling up and down on Facebook randomly to pass time. However, only 36% admitted to stalking on Facebook. Moreover 7% people message others to like their posts/pictures. Also, 12% have resorted to buying custom username. 15% did agree that they become aggressive or restless due to lack of Facebook usage. Moreover, 15% admitted to the usage of Facebook to forget about their problems, and 23% have tried to cut down on Facebook usage without success. So correlation of stress with Facebook is there.

Conclusion

So we conclude that Facebook addiction is not as widespread as everyone thinks to be. However, some people (very small fraction) do show extreme signs of obsession towards Facebook.

References

Gilbert, K. (2010, December 13). The Psychology of Facebook OCD. Retrieved January 12, 2018, from http://www.psychologytoday.com/blog/insight-is-2020/201012/Facebook-OCD

Gilbert, K. (2010, December 13). The Psychology of Facebook OCD. Retrieved

January 12, 2018, from http://www.psychologytoday.com/blog/insight-is-2020/201012/Facebook-OCD

Manuel-Logan, R. (2011, April 29). Do You Suffer From Facebook Addiction Disorder? Retrieved January 12, 2018, from http://allFacebook.com/do-you-suffer-from-Facebook-addiction-disorder_b41648

Paddock, C. (2015, June 22). Facebook Addiction - New Psychological Scale. Retrieved January 12, 2018, from http://www.medicalnewstoday.com/articles/245251.php

Obsessive-compulsive disorder (OCD). (2016, September 17). Retrieved January 12, 2018, from http://www.mayoclinic.org/diseases-conditions/OCD/basics/symptoms/con-20027827

Obsessive-Compulsive Facebook Disorder (OCFD). (n.d.). Retrieved January 12, 2018, from http://www.urbandictionary.com/define.php?term=Obsessive-Compulsive%2BFacebook%2BDisorder%2B%28OCFD%29

Appendix

Questionnaire

<u>Part- I</u>

1) Choose your age bracket
    a) 13-18
    b) 19-25
    c) >25
2) How many hours do you spend on Facebook in a day?
    a) <1hr
    b) 1 - 2 Hrs
    c) 2- 4 Hrs
    d) 4- 5 Hrs
    e) >5hrs
3) How long have you been signed up for Facebook?
    a) < 1 year
    b) 1- 2 years
    c) 3 - 5 years
    d) > 5years
4) How many Facebook friends do you have?
    a) I don't know(if you're not sure)
    b) <10
    c) 11 - 50
    d) 51 - 100
    e) 101 - 500

    f)   501 - 1000
    g)   1001 - 5000
    h)   > 5000

5) How many photos are you tagged in?
    a)   I don't know
    b)   tens
    c)   100 -499
    d)   500-999
    e)   thousands
    f)   > thousands

6) When you sit down at a computer, what do you usually check first?
    a)   email
    b)   news
    c)   twitter
    d)   Facebook
    e)   other

<u>Part -II</u>

Answer the following questions answer with a yes or a no.:

1. Do you have a smartphone?
2. Do you start your day by logging in to Facebook to check for notifications?
3. Do you often update your Facebook status?
4. Do you fantasize about making the next great Facebook status update?
5. Is Facebook the only mode of communication between your family and friends?
6. Have you enrolled in a costly photography course so that your Facebook pics become the talk of your circle?
7. Have you resorted to paying off strangers to become your Facebook friend so that your number defies all logic?
8. Whenever you fight with your significant other, do you feel compelled to change your Facebook relationship status?
9. Do you use Facebook late at night (11 pm and later)?
10. Do you get annoyed when someone doesn't upload and tag photos to Facebook after a social outing?
11. Do you stalk anyone on FB?
12. Do you randomly scroll up and down your homepage even if no work is needed to do?
13. Have you ever met a new 'in real life' friend from Facebook or gone on a date from Facebook (at any time in our life)?
14. Do feel extremely depressed if someone gives negative posts about you or write negative comments about your posts, pictures etc?
15. Do you message your friends to like your post/ pictures etc.?
16. Did you choose a custom username?
17. Do you become restless or troubled if you are prohibited from using Facebook?
18. Do you use Facebook to forget about personal problems?
19. Have you ever tried to cut down on the use of Facebook without success?

Chapter 6

Report on Facebook vs. Leisure Activities

Sushmita Sinha, Dibyangana, & Maya Menon

Introduction

Facebook allows individuals to meet people with similar interests and connect with their friends on their social networks. To create a social networking website Facebook account, an individual has to create a profile with demographic data and relational data, and the humongous amount of data from users' profiles has created a fertile and attractive source of data for researchers. The increasing popularity of Facebook has some impacts on friendship, information sharing, and leisure activities. According to the EDUCAR annual survey of undergraduate students' use of information technology, the percentage of students who use social network sites has increased from 81.6% in 2007 to 90.4% in 2010 and students used social network sites to connect with friends, share photos, find out more about people, communicate with classmates and plan or invite people to events.

Leisure activities

Many people spend their leisure activities in many ways like playing, watching tv, reading books. According to the 2011 survey, total average leisure and sports time for Americans was 5.19 h per day, exercising. There are some people who spend their leisure time in social networking like Facebook, which consisted of 18 min of participating in sports, exercise and recreation, 42 min for socializing and communicating, 2.75 h for watching TV, 18 min for reading, 18 min for relaxing and thinking, 26 min for playing games and using the computer for leisure, and 25 min for other leisure activities. Overall, the times used for watching TV and playing games and using the computer for leisure had increased, but the times used for socializing and reading had decreased since 2003.

There is a need to focus on the circumstantial statistical reports which have been provided through different online sources. The need to study the sources through survey reports of Facebook usage versus the leisure activities and a poll by following factors namely:

1. Gaming
2. Applications
3. Profile updates
4. Chatting Prediction with online friends
5. Sharing of pictures and videos
6. Liking social pages and joining groups

Methodology

It may be considered that a total of 100 people were studied and the report comes out to be following a regular relationship between no of Facebook users and people who preferably would be choosing daily leisure activities.

Results & Discussion

The survey reports are as follows:

Here, the blue bars are for the representation of Facebook and its characteristics also the red bars are for the competing Leisure activities:

The histogram is comparing each question and the poll rating for each one of them. The varying responses for each of the other questions have been represented below:

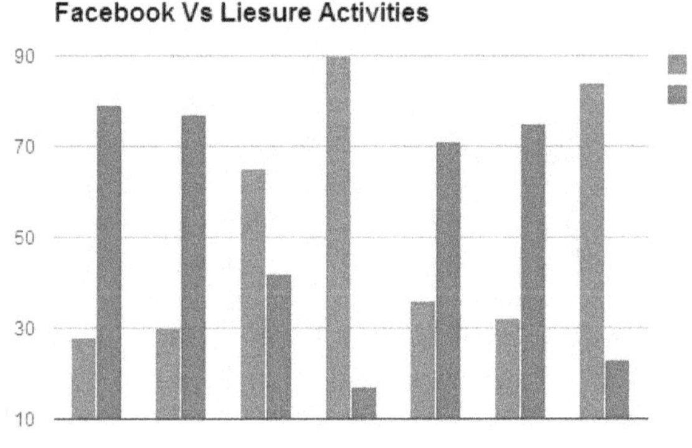

Figure 1- Facebook versus the leisure activities

As it can view and can be studied from the graph present below, no of people choosing for a great joy of surfing on the net for hours are statistically less in number.

It may be statistically inferred that minimum number of people choosing leisure activities over the usual times when being busy with attending Facebook normally also major time proportion has been allotted to the Facebook usage and lack of leisure activities which may be remarkably inferred as a replacement to the other here 90 of them have answered they like to rather log in to Facebook as their time passage.

As it has been found from the statistics that majorly 65 people out of 100 logins to Facebook only to read their news feeds cutting down other leisure activities when they are free of all other works.

When talking about choosing leisure activities over the Facebook usage 84 out of 100 people indulge themselves in online Facebook games and other visiting sites. The statistics read out as per the survey says that 79 out of 100 people under the circle of scrutiny prefer being online as compared to normal spending time with friends. The following statistics also describes the Facebook usage and amount of time spent on leisure activities. Most of the people spend time using Facebook through mobile phone as there it is the era of smartphones and works made easy.

Conclusion

The inference that can be drawn from the following statistical report is that due to the increase in the popularity and dependency on social networking sites the present generations that have been put under the study have developed a new interaction platform. It may be said that the occurrence of Facebook usage and characteristics also statistically has been growing these days. The importance of leisure activities such as reading books and many other is going through a replacement with an online new world on which people nowadays are interacting.

The dependency of people on their relationship with other people has now become a matter of just one click go. The world is getting connected and constantly changing. Facebook has now become a way of expression, and thus it is getting instant with one touch on smartphones. Ii has also affected the conclusive of all the leisure activities which were once a way of recreation. The biggest world may be referred to like Facebook, and the leisure activities as per the study and survey are statistically losing popularity in going with a replacement.

References

Amichai-Hamburger, Y., & Hayat, Z. (2011). The impact of the Internet on the social lives of users: A representative sample from 13 countries. *Computers in Human Behavior*, 27(2011), 585–589.

Bureau of Labor Statistics, (2012). American time use survey-2003–2011 results, retrieved on May 10, 2013. <http://www.bls.gov/news.release/pdf/atus.pdf>.

Facebook, 2013, Facebook statistics, retrieved on May 10, 2013. <http://newsroom.fb.com/Key-Facts>.

Hew, K. (2011). Students' and teachers' use of Facebook. *Computers in Human Behavior*, 27(2011), 662–676.

Smith, S., & Caruso, J. (2010). The ECAR Study of Undergraduate Students and Information Technology, 2010. Boulder, Colorado: EDUCAUSE Center for Applied Research.

Appendix

Questionnaire

1. How often do you use Facebook?
    i.   more than 5 hours per day
    ii. more than 7 hours per day
    iii. more than 10 hours
    iv. Other:
2. How much weekly do you spend on leisure activities?
    i.   2 hours
    ii. 3-6 hours
    iii. more than 10 hours
3. What type of leisure activities do you like more?
    i.   Listening to music
    ii. Playing games
    iii. Reading books
    iv. Watching tv series
    v.   Other:
4. How often do you use your mobile phone (or someone else's mobile phone) to access the internet or visit social network sites?
    i.   Several times a day
    ii. About once a day
    iii. A few times a week
    iv. Less than once a week
    v.   Never, I don't have access to a device with this service
5. What type of leisure activities do you prefer on social networking sites?
    i.   Games
    ii. Chatting with friends
    iii. Updating your status

      iv.   Sharing pictures and videos
      v.   Other:

6. How often do you update your status?
      i.   Once in a week
      ii.   About Everyday
      iii.   Once in a month
      iv.   Once in a year

7. Do you prefer being online than attending usual hangouts with your college friends?
      i.   Yes
      ii.   No

8. Do you share an update only on likes and comments?
      i.   Yes
      ii.   No

9. What kind of game applications do you prefer?
      i.   Self-defending
      ii.   Involving opposite parties
      iii.   Group play
      iv.   Other:

10. Do you login to your Facebook account just to look into your news feeds?
      i.   Yes
      ii.   No

Chapter 7

Does Facebook Promote Narcissism?

Sruthy Lekha B & Angeline Surekha S

Introduction

Narcissism

Narcissism describes the character trait of self-love, based on self-image or ego. In psychology and psychiatry, excessive narcissism is recognized as a severe personality dysfunction or personality disorder, most characteristically narcissistic personality disorder also referred to as NPD.

Sigmund Freud (1994) believed that some narcissism is an essential part of all of us from birth and was the first to use the term in reference to psychology.

Narcissism is a disorder or mental illness that causes a lot of pain for both the narcissist and those who love him. It is the narcissist's refusal to accept responsibility for his behavior and actions that cause so much pain for others. It is his projecting his repressed feelings of self-loathing onto others and lashing out at others as a sort of dumping or discarding of those pent up emotions that erode the self-worth of his victims.

Narcissism begins in childhood, as a normal part of development but it becomes a coping mechanism for those who never outgrow it. They construct a sophisticated fantasy world to protect them from the real world and its consequences.

Facebook usage and narcissism

Facebook is one of the most popular websites in the world with over 600 million users (Ahmad, 2011). Those who use Facebook enjoy many benefits.

Examination of the interpersonal possibilities offered by Facebook as well as the limited extant research suggests several tentative hypotheses about Facebook behaviors and narcissism. Therefore, they are predicted to have a high friend count given their drive to seek attention from as many people as possible. If they are seeking a wider audience, they are also predicted to accept friend requests from strangers because they would be seeking an audience rather than using Facebook to engage in social interaction with existing friends. They may also attempt to gain the attention of their audience by frequently offering new content. Posting status updates, posting pictures of themselves, and changing their profile are all methods of using Facebook to focus attention on the self. (Carpenter, 2011)

Methodology

Sampling and Data Collection

This descriptive study was conducted by using a survey method. The population comprised of students of age group 18-21. A questionnaire was created, and a survey was taken online with help from docs.google.com at the following link:
https://docs.google.com/a/vit.ac.in/forms/d/10UPQdnaCF0lGC0oIKCrImVG sSngfj9nZF9F_j2i3Jpk/viewform

The questionnaire was answered by random students, of the age group mentioned, from different colleges. A total of 106 responses were received.

Data Analysis Techniques

The questions were framed, and feedbacks were received in Microsoft Excel. A descriptive analysis of the data received was also done on Microsoft Excel.

Results and Discussion

Number of male and female respondents

male	53	49.5%
female	54	50.5%

How often do you check Facebook?

very often (several times a day)	30	28.3%
often (2-3 times a day)	39	36.8%
sometimes (once in a few days)	27	25.5%

rarely	**10**	9.4%

Do you accept unknown friend requests on Facebook?

yes	**16**	15.1%
no	**90**	84.9%

How frequently do you update status/ share pictures?

quite often	**6**	5.7%
often	**12**	11.3%
not so often	**79**	74.5%
never	**9**	8.5%

"I use Facebook to show-off."

strongly disagree	**33**	31.1%
disagree	**52**	49.1%
agree	**21**	19.8%
strongly agree	**0**	0%

An average number of likes on status/pics?

cannot specify	**62**	63.3%
Other	**36**	36.7%

Use Facebook to express identity/opinion

strongly disagree	**7**	6.7%
disagree	**39**	37.1%
agree	**56**	53.3%

strongly agree	**3**	2.9%

"I use Facebook to communicate with people I know."

strongly disagree	**1**	0.9%
disagree	**7**	6.6%
agree	**69**	65.1%
strongly agree	**29**	27.4%

"I use Facebook to make friends with strangers."

strongly disagree	**47**	44.8%
disagree	**34**	32.4%
agree	**22**	21%
strongly agree	**2**	1.9%

Tick as appropriate (last column indicates score to determine narcissistic character):

Question	Count	score	
compliments embarrass me	27	25.2%	0
I like being complimented	80	74.8%	1
I like to have authority over people	30	40%	1
I don't mind following orders	49	65.3%	0
I like to be the center of attention	42	51.2%	1
being center of attention makes me uncomfortable	42	51.2%	0
I will never be satisfied until I get all that I deserve.	23	26.4%	1
I will never be satisfied until I get all that I deserve.	23	26.4%	1
I take my satisfaction as it comes.	66	75.9%	0

How often do you update your status/picture on Facebook

Very often	often	Not so often	never
3	2	1	0

The narcissistic score of each individual was calculated as 1-4 (by summing up the scores mentioned above) where 4 indicates highly narcissistic individual. The Responses to the question on frequency of status updation was scored as shown in the table above.

Correlation between narcissistic scores and frequency was obtained using Microsoft Excel

The correlation coefficient was found to 0.065

Conclusion

From the results, we can see that most of the respondents agreed to use Facebook often or very often indicating that Facebook usage is on the rise and it could impact behavior. Many factors could influence narcissism, but our study focuses on the influence of Facebook on narcissism. The correlation coefficient, between the frequency of Facebook status updation and the collective score for narcissism, was calculated. It was found to be 0.065. Therefore we can conclude that there is a weak correlation between Facebook usage and narcissism. Facebook does not promote narcissism, rather narcissistic individuals use Facebook as one of the ways showcasing themselves.

Limitations

This study is limited to only a hundred respondents, and wider sample range would give a more conclusive result. Also, due to some constraints, only very few questions from the standard narcissistic personality inventory were selected for the survey.

References

Carpenter, C. J. (2012). Self-Promotional and Anti-Social Behavior on Facebook Survey. *PsycTESTS Dataset*. doi:10.1037/t36986-000

Marshall, T. C., Lefringhausen, K., & Ferenczi, N. (2015). The Big Five, self-esteem, and narcissism as predictors of the topics people write about in Facebook status updates. *Personality and Individual Differences, 85*, 35-40. doi:10.1016/j.paid.2015.04.039

Mckinney, B. C., Kelly, L., & Duran, R. L. (2012). Narcissism or Openness?: College Students' Use of Facebook and Twitter. *Communication Research Reports, 29*(2), 108-118. doi:10.1080/08824096.2012.666919

Chapter 8

Stress Level of Using Facebook

Shardul Mishra, Chirag Tripathi, & Shrey Sharma

Introduction

Facebook: A marked innovation by Mark

It has been ten years since a Harvard sophomore named Mark Zuckerberg created a website called Facebook.com to let his classmates find their friends online. They did and so done by every seventh person of huge world population, ranging from farmers in India to the pop stars in South Korea. It is worthless to say that Facebook is now an integral part of the life style of a person belonging to social. Not only has this social networking site created the opportunity in being contacts with one's favourite community, his likes, relatives, friends and so much but as general or particularly in India, Facebook has played a very important role in political revolutions also. No matter whether it is Anna Hazare's movements or government formation by AAP in Delhi and the story continues.

Why such a large use?

It is not the only site that provides communication across social, the present arena of the Internet is full of such social networking sites, but the question is here: why only Facebook? It is because of its simplicity in use, and compatibility across multiple devices like mobiles, i-phones, etc. Also, its popularity is governed by its service of quick and easy sign-up method, not requiring any specialty user. "One of the things Facebook has been good at is that it's very easy to use and understand," said Paul Levinson, professor of communications and media studies at Fordham University. "It's a much friendlier system than any email system."

Where is the Problem? Factors relating Facebook with stress

Because of the same, that is its simplicity in use, and compatibility across multiple devices, range, and frequency of Facebook uses and psychological effect are subject matters to social study. A huge amount of Facebook certainly creates some kind of psychological impacts on the user, which may be caused by any irrelevant information through the community he is connected, long time off-connectivity, slow network access, long time chatting, unauthorized access to an imposter, unwanted comments on his likes or dislikes, etc. Though these factors are very common they afford very great effect over a large number of people. A survey data[1] suggest that Facebook could be a new source of psychological stress. The survey examined Undergraduate college student perceptions of Facebook use and incidence of upper respiratory infections (URIs). In survey it was hypothesized that subjects with more diverse networks (i.e., more friends on Facebook) would have fewer URIs than their less diverse counterparts; that subjects reporting Facebook-induced stress would be more susceptible to URIs; and that subjects with more diverse networks who report Facebook-induced stress would be less susceptible to URIs than subjects with less diverse social networks who reported Facebook-induced stress. The effects of Facebook-induced stress on the incidence of URI varied across the social network size, such that, the impact of stress on the URI incidence rate increased with the size of the social network. This suggests an association between Facebook use, psychological stress, and health. Another conclusion[2] made by researchers conducted with Bachelor of Science in nursing program from a government university in Samar, Philippines, says that time spent on Facebook increases depression and anxiety score. But together with a factor of time, the quality of Facebook also use matters, for example, if anyhow user spent most of the time in making his organisation popular, then it is his job to do, in that case, psychological parameters are referred to complicated situation of his mind. Thus our intended aim is to show how use in reference to quantity as well the quality of Facebook contributes one's level of stress. In our study, use of Facebook (use in reference to time and type) is an independent variable that gives contribution in developing stress level of the user (Dependent variable).

Stratified Sampling•

Subdivide the population into at least two different subgroups that share the same characteristics, and then draw a sample from

•A design in which every set of every factor appears with every setting of every other factor is a full factorial design.

Full Factorial Design

– e.g., A common experimental design is one with all input factors set at two levels each. These levels are called `high' and `low' or `+1' and `-1', respectively. Design with all possible high/low combinations of all the input factors is called a full factorial design in two levels.

Dot Plot

Consists of a graph in which each data value is plotted as a point (or dot) along with a scale of values. Dots representing equal values are stacked

Comparative Objective

If there are one or several factors under investigation, but the primary goal of the experiment is to make a conclusion about one a-priori important factor, (in the presence of, and/or in spite of the existence of the other factors), and the question of interest is whether or not that factor is "significant", (i.e., whether or not there is a significant change in the response for different levels of that factor), then it is a *comparative problem* and a *comparative design* solution is needed.

Test of Hypothesis

- The null hypothesis, H0: $\mu =.$ 125cms
- Alternate hypothesis,
- –Ha : $\mu \neq 125$ cms, Ha : $\mu < 125$ cms, Ha : $\mu > 125$ cms
- Test criterion *–t and z test*
- Acceptance/ Rejection Region & Critical Value
- Level of significance (α) -Type I error (0.05)
- Confidence Level
- One-tailed & Two-tailed test
- Degrees of freedom: n-1

Result and Discussion

In case of stress symptoms, only 12 out of 71 accepted that they do not do anything other than Facebook. All other accepted to be involved in other works like eating net surfing and studying. No one accepted to have high saliva formation during Facebook. 38 out of 71 accepted to have abnormal impulse rate on Facebook. Most people 31/71 accepted to have an overnight chat. An equal number of people selected that it gives cheer and stress. Most of the people have deactivated their account either once or more than once. Only 1 out of 71 selected that they never want to log out figuring out your depression.

Conclusion

Seeing the results of response we can say that people feel stress when they are on Facebook, but they don't want to be free from it. It seems as-as if they enjoy the stress, like they are addicted to it. They know that it is destroying their time but they do not logout of it. Hence sometimes they deactivate their account.

References

Campisi, J., Bynog, P., Mcgeehee, H., Oakland, J., Quirk, S., Taga, C., & Taylor, M. (n.d.). Facebook, stress, and incidence of upper respiratory infection in undergraduate college students. *PsycEXTRA Dataset.* doi:10.1037/e545662013-062

Appendix
Questionnaire:
The stress level of Using Facebook

Question 1: How long you're on Facebook?
A.   Less than 6 months   o
B.   Less than a year   o
C.   Less than 3 years   o
D.   More than 3 years   o

Question 1: How much time you spend on Facebook?
A.   Less than 5 hours   o
B.   More than 5 but less than 10 hours   o
C.   More than mentioned   o

Question 2: Do you notice any change in your behaviour between the time you're online and offline?
A. None   o
B.   Slightly   o
C.   Considerable   o
D.   Very Much   o

Question 3: When do you feel upset?
A.   If not used Facebook for more than the number of hours   o
B.   If not used Facebook for more than the number of days   o
C.   If used Facebook for more than the number of hours   o

Question 4: How many times you want be just log out, figuring out your depression?
A.   Very often   o
B.   Once or twice over a weak   o
C.   Rarely   o
D.   Never   o

Question 5: Joining Facebook has (in reference towards normal psychological behaviour)
A.   Increased your attention   o
B.   Decreased your attention   o
C.   Made you confuse   o
D.   Made you clear   o

Question 6: According to you, Facebook makes you
A.   Cheerful   o
B.   Social   o
C.   Limited   o

Question 7: How much time you've deactivated your account regarding feeling insecure and making you under strain?
A.   Once since you created account   o
B.   More than once, since you created account   o
(If possible, please mention the number of times you did so……..)

C. Rarely   o
D. Never   o

Question 9: Sometimes you visit verities of pages; they may contain some information that may give you bad impression and stress, how many times you've gone through such situation?

A. Once   o
B. More than Once   o
C. Rarely   o
D. Never   o

Question 10: You spent your most of your time on Facebook in

A. Visiting Pages   o
B. Chatting   o
C. Finding friends   o
D. Gaming   o

Question 11: According to you, chatting gives you,

A. Always feel of cheers   o
B. Sometimes stress   o
C. Always stress   o
D. Sometimes feel of cheers   o

Question 12: You chat,

A. Every time you're online   o
B. Less than the time you're online   o
C. Few hours you're online   o
D. None, you always turn chat off   o

Question 13: Overnight chatting occurs,

A. Very frequent   o
B. Rarely   o
C. Once or twice in a month   o
D. Never   o

Question 14: Have you ever noticed pulse rate after a long time use of Facebook? It is,

A. High   o
B. Low   o
C. Normal   o

Question 15: What other activities you like to do when you're online?

A. Eating   o
B. Internet surfing   o
C. Study (although it is very confusing)   o
D. Nothing than usual   o

Question 16: Rate of salivary amylase production during ongoing Facebook

A. High   o
B. Low   o
C. Normal   o

Thanks for giving your time on this survey!

Chapter 9

Effects of Facebook on Personal Life

Ayushi

Introduction

Studying emotions has been the centre of attraction for psychologists. This kind of study requires observation of emotional demonstrations. Collection of emotional data is a crucial step towards the development of study. Facebook is nowadays an integral part of everyone's life. Almost everyone in their college life spends a lot of time on social networking sites. Especially, when we talk about engineering students in VIT, they are one step ahead in these activities. According to recent studies, Facebook has major effects on the personal lives of people. These effects can be both positive and negative. These effects may include low self-esteem, low academic and emotional adjustment, relationship problems, self-confidence, and motivation. Some of their findings suggest that the more time spent on Facebook is related to a greater tendency toward narcissistic behaviors among teenagers. Also, it has been discovered that young adults that spend excessive amounts of time on Facebook show more signs of other psychological disorders, including antisocial behaviors, mania, and aggressive tendencies.

On the other hand, research has shown that, despite the numerous negative effects, Facebook can help young adults to express their virtual empathy and facilitate socialization among introverted teens. Also, social networking can provide tools for teaching in compelling ways that engage young students. It seems, like most things in life, everything in moderation is best.

Results

Pie charts- summary

1. Which age group do you belong to?

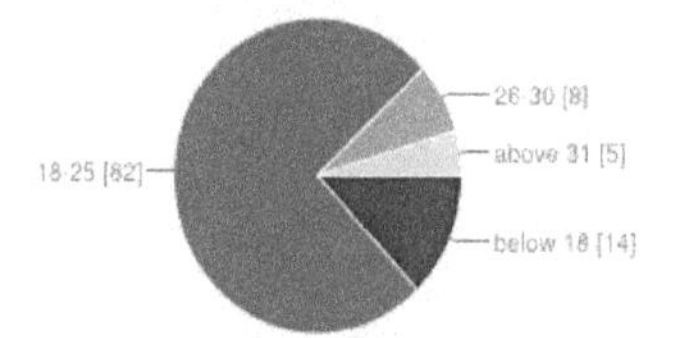

below 18	14	13%
18-25	82	75%
26-30	8	7%
above 31	5	5%

2. How often do you visit Facebook?

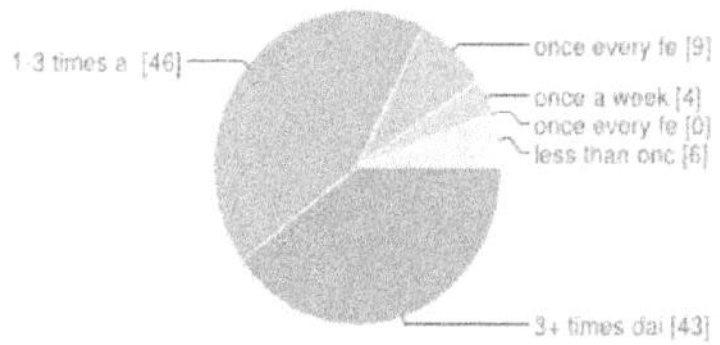

3+ times daily	43	40%
1-3 times a day	46	43%
once every few days	9	8%
once a week	4	4%
once every few weeks	0	0%
less than once a month	6	6%

Discussion

According to already existing research with sample size 119, it was seen that respondents were predominantly female (68%) and the largest age group ranged from 22–24 years old (27%). Half of the respondents had their Facebook account for 2 years, and 37% checked this account daily, with 25% checking it three times a day and 23% checking it five times a day. On average, half of the respondents were spending up to 15 minutes each time they use Facebook, while 20% spent up to 30 minutes and 20% spent up to 5 minutes. Over a quarter (29%) reported that their Facebook account is always open or active when they are online. Almost 18% reported personally experiencing negative effects of Facebook, such as unwanted advances, stalking, and harassment, damaging gossip or rumor, or data theft. 47% said they restricted access to their profile because they are generally cautious, and 38% because they had heard "some concerning stories." Most respondents (83%) reported that Facebook helps them interact with friends and other people.

Conclusion

From the above discussions and the plotted graphs, it can be thus concluded that Facebook is predominantly used by the people belonging to the age group 18-25 years. Also, fem Facebook has both positive and negative effects on a person's life. Positive effects may include better social and emotional adjustments while negative effects include low self-esteem and academic problems etc. It is thus rightly said that 'like most things in life, everything in moderation is best.'

Appendix

Questionnaire

1. Which age group do you belong to?

    i.   below 18

    ii.   18-25

    iii.   26-30

    iv.   above 31

2. How often do you visit Facebook?

    i.   3+ times daily

    ii.   1-3 times a day

    iii.   once every few days

    iv.   once a week

    v.   once every few weeks

    vi.   less than once a month

3. How many friends do have on Facebook?

    i.   less than 200

    ii.   between 200 to 400

    iii.   between 400 to 600

    iv.   between 600 to 800

    v.   between 800 to 1000

    vi.   more than 1000

4. How often do you update any aspect of your profile on Facebook?

    i.   3+ times daily

    ii.   1-3 times a day

    iii.   once every few days

    iv.   once a week

    v.   once every few weeks

5. Do you consider Facebook a significant part of your life?

    i.   yes

    ii.   no

    iii.   can't say

6. Do the results of your observations of their profile impact how you interact with a person in the future?

    i.   always

    ii.   often

    iii.   sometimes

    iv.   rarely

    v.   never

7. What is your comfort level indicating your relationship status when (if) you are in a relationship?

    i.   more comfortable

    ii.   less comfortable

    iii.   no difference

    iv.   not sure

8. Is Facebook an accurate portrayal of people's true personalities?

    i.   yes

    ii.   no

    iii.   maybe

9. Do you consider Facebook similar to a dating service?

    i.   yes

    ii.   no

    iii.   sometimes

10. How often do you meet your Facebook friends in 'real life'?

    i.   quite often

    ii.   sometimes

    iii.   never

11. Do you add your family members in your friend list?

    i.   yes

    ii.   no

    iii.   some of them

12. How do you feel when your family member views your Facebook profile?

    i.   scared

    ii.   offended

    iii.   neutral

    iv.   can't say

13. Do you add people who you don't know personally?

    i.   yes

    ii.   no

    iii.   sometimes

14. Do you feel free to express your feelings or share your secrets to your online friends?

    i.   yes

    ii.   no

    iii.   maybe

    iv.   depends on the person

15. Did you tell something very personal to any of your online friends and regret it later?

    i.   yes, quite often

    ii.   once or twice

    iii.   no, i trust only very close friends

    iv.   never told anything personal to online friends

16. What is generally your mood when you are browsing online?

    i.   happy

    ii.   sad

    iii.   angry

    iv.   neutral

    v.   excited

    vi.   bored

17. How often do you come online when you have other important work to do?

    i.   never

    ii.   rarely

    iii.   sometimes

    iv.   most of the times

18. Will your opinion about a person change if you don't like his/her profile?

    i.   definitely

    ii.   maybe

    iii.   depends on the person

    iv.   never thought about it

19. Do you feel comfortable sharing your Facebook password with anyone?

    i.   never

    ii.   yes, sometimes

    iii.   maybe

    iv.   only to someone very close

20. Would you like to meet in person or date people who you met online?

    i.   yes, you wouldn't mind

    ii.   no, you can't trust them

    iii.   maybe, depends on the person

    iv.   haven't thought about it

Chapter 10

The Difference in Psychological Impact of Mainstream Social Media Trends on the Sexes

Shalaka Sathish Wate, Mayank Kumar Modi, & Pallavi Sinha Roy

Introduction

Narcissistic Personality Disorder (NPD) and Histrionic Personality Disorder (HPD) are both cluster B personality disorders. NPD affects around 1% of the population, and the affected individuals have heightened feelings of self-admiration and self-importance and felt that they always deserve to be the center of attention. According to the symptoms of NPD defined by Diagnostic and Statistical Manual of Mental Disorders, 5th Edition (DSM-5), the affected individuals greatly lack empathy, and they maintain superficial relationships, lacking depth and intimacy. Disorder (NPD) is characterized by excessive preoccupation with personal adequacy, power, prestige, vanity, and a lack of empathy [1]. It is a severe form of egocentrism. In the past few decades, NPD has been receiving growing attention as a personality disorder and while carrying out a "subject" search on PsychINFO (2013), using the term "Narcissistic Personality Disorder", 1573 hits came about. By contrast, when a similar search was carried out with "Histrionic Personality Disorder", only about 405 hits were present. Despite HPD being a clinical syndrome, it has garnered less attention in research and clinical literature, when compared to other cluster B personality disorders [2]. American Psychiatric Association has defined HPD as a personality disorder with early onset in adulthood. The affected individuals are flirtatious, inappropriately sexually suggestive, and have the constant requirement for approval. They are extremely vivacious, dramatic and they possess excessive attention seeking emotions. Despite of there being various symptoms of HPD, there is no stand-alone, freely accessible clinical measure for HPD symptoms, which explains the absence of meticulous research carried out on HPD. Although HPD and NPD are two distinct personality disorders, they have few overlapping symptoms, thereby, paving the way for possible co-morbidity.

In this paper, we attempt to correlate the frequency and motivation behind the usage of social media networks to the occurrence of NPD and HPD respectively in young individuals. Social networking media has been seen to pervade more and more realms of our lives every passing day. This pervasion is manifesting its effects in the form of alterations in a person's concept of self, persistent emotions, behaviour, and social relations. Predispositions to certain personality disorders have been established to be a partial function of a person's gender. Prevalent gender stereotypes in today's society could also increase a person's susceptibility to specific personality disorders. Standard tests have been used in this paper to diagnose the occurrences of HPD and NPD in people as well as to determine the number of people that are predisposed to the disorders. The standard tests that have been used for NPD and HPD are Narcissistic Personality Inventory (NPI-16) and Brief Histrionic Personality Scale (BHPS) respectively. NPI-16 has been derived from NPI-40 and constructs and validates a one-dimensional and shorter measure of narcissism. NPI-16 has been specifically preferred in situations in which the usage of a lengthier measure would be impractical, and the respondents might not be too willing to answer such a lengthy survey of 40 questions [3]. For HPD, BHPS standardized test has been used as it is reliable, brief, easy to score and freely available to the research and clinical community. The other tests for HPD, like MCMI-III nor MMPI-2 scales, have not been used as they are problematic and they consist of large personality measures that are pretty lengthy as well as costly and in the case of MMPI-2 histrionic scale, scoring proves to be inconvenient [2].

This study aims to characterize as well as quantify the social media behavior of young individuals through the scoring of a general questionnaire, while simultaneously evaluating them for the occurrence of NPD and HPD through the aforementioned standardized index tests, followed by an analysis and intuitive linkage of all the three scores in these individuals. A concretized linkage between these scores will enable us to understand the social manifestation of NPD and HPD in the virtual world of internet.

Methodology

Participants

Participants (N = 192) were students from VIT University, Vellore from different streams and majors. The survey was conducted online via google forms link: https://docs.google.com/forms/d/1KgBOXwDkkMxHGC_gsrEcs4LeZ51I4h0 2ZJFccxyQpyQ/viewform

The survey was based on multiple-choice questions only with single and multi-choice questions. On the whole, the participants (N = 192) ranged in age from 17 to 27 years (M = 21.20, SD = 3.45). Participants included 114 males and 78 females who portray a mixed set of Indian population comprising of North

Indians, South Indian, and others.

Hypothesis: People suffering from clinically significant/borderline NPD or HPD are more likely to exploit social media sites as a platform for dispensing the typical symptoms of their respective disorder. Such platforms are conducive to the people with narcissistic and histrionic tendencies.

Measures

Narcissistic Personality Inventory (NPI) - 16. The NPI – 16 [3] which is a shorter measure derived from NPI – 40 (Raskin & Terry, 1988) is a 16-item self-report assessment that measures trait narcissism. NPI-16 was designed for situations where time limitations and participant uncooperativeness are significant concerns. The NPI-16 is one of the most commonly employed standardized measures for narcissism in non-clinical settings and has been extensively evaluated for its face, internal, discriminant, and predictive validity. The mean NPI score in the current sample was 4.88 (SD = 2.87).

Brief Histrionic Personality Scale (BHPS). The BHPS [2] is a 36-item self-report assessment that measures trait histrionics. The BHPS is a recently designed measure of histrionics in the field of social personality and has been widely evaluated with a gamut of criteria including confirmatory factor analysis, test-retest validity, and test reports. The initial 36-items have been narrowed down to an 11-item inventory with considerable reliability for short-term non-clinical studies [2]. The mean BHPS score in the current sample was 24.09 (SD = 5.20).

General Questionnaire (GQ). A self-made 15-item multiple-choice questionnaire was designed to measure the social media presence of a participant and different social media parameters such as selfies, hashtags, Facebook likes, use of photo editing software, status updates, tagging friends, posting answers on Quora, etc., were quantified and scored. Questions were both qualitative and analytical with some of them having specific options directly linked either to narcissism or histrionics. The GQ was scored separately for NPD and HPD comparison based on the specific options devised. The mean NPD-GQ and HPD-GQ scores are 13.96 (SD = 5.91) and 13.58 (SD = 5.98), respectively.

Procedure

The NPI-16 scores and the NPD-GQ scores of the sample population were compared and analyzed to establish the relationship between them and also ascertain the credibility of NPD-GQ test data. Chi-squared (goodness of fit) analysis was performed to assess the relationship between three frequency classes that are normal, borderline, and clinical segments of both the test. The same analysis was performed to establish the credibility of HPD-GQ and relationship among BHSP and HPD-GQ tests. All data arrangement and analysis were done using χ MS Excel software. Scatter was made to extrapolate a relation between the standardized and the GQ tests for both the disorders.

Results

NPI-16 and NPD-GQ test analysis

Chi-square test was performed between the number of participants falling under each category of NPI-16 scores and NPD-GQ scores for comparison. The χ^2 value obtained was 0.389 at $p < .05$ for degree of freedom = 1. The score is well below the specific standard chi-square distribution score leading to acceptance of the null hypothesis. Thus, we can conclude that there is no significant difference between the observed frequencies and the expected frequencies.

The mean NPI score observed in the participants was 4.88 with SD = 2.87. The mean NPD-GQ score observed was 13.97 with SD = 5.91. According to the NPI test results, of the total sample 79.69% participants under the normal (score from 0-7) category with a mean score = 3.75 (SD = 1.90) and 20.31% of the participants under the combined (borderline and clinical together: score above 7) category with mean = 9.28 (SD = 1.44) as shown in Fig 1. In correspondence, according to the NPD-GQ test results 82.81% participants under the normal (score from 0-21) category had a mean score = 13.90 (SD = 5.95) and 17.91% of the participants under the combined (borderline and clinical together: score above 21) category with mean = 15.84 (SD = 5.35) as shown in Fig 2.

The mean value of the NPD-GQ test scores from normal category to the combined (with comparatively high social media presence and usage of social networks) category increased only slightly from 13.90 to 15.84 when compared to the high increase across categories in the mean values of NPI test scores from 3.75 to 9.28.

Out of the 153 participants in the normal NPI score category, a total of 14.38% were in the combined category for NPD-GQ scores which is a low but notable amount (Fig 5.). Similarly, the borderline NPI population with 35 participants had 25.71% (Fig 6.) of its share in the combined category, and the clinical NPI population of 4 participants had 50% in the borderline category (Fig 7.) with no respondents in the clinical level category in the NPD-GQ test. These relatively small values of risk individuals in the three categories of NPI test scores account for the low rise in mean score across categories in the NPD-GQ test.

BHSP and HPD-GQ test analysis

The χ^2 value obtained was 0.508 at $p < .05$ for degree of freedom = 1. The score is well below the specific standard chi-square distribution score leading to acceptance of the null hypothesis. Thus, we can conclude that there is no significant difference between the observed frequencies and the expected frequencies.

Overall, participants were found to have a mean BHSP score of 24.09 with SD = 5.20. The mean HPD-GQ score was found to be 13.63 with SD = 5.98. Basing on the BHSP test results, from the whole sample 84.38% of the respondents within the normal (score from 11-29) category had a mean score = 22.56 (SD = 3.94) and 15.63% of the participants within the combined (borderline and clinical together: score above 29) category had mean = 32.43 (SD = 2.64) as shown in Fig 3. In relation, the HPD-GQ test included 85.42% participants under the normal (score from 0-21) category had a mean score = 13.34 (SD = 5.88) and 14.58% of the participants under the combined (borderline and clinical together: score above 21) category with mean = 15.70 (SD = 6.07) as shown in Fig 4.

The mean HPD-GQ test score value from normal category to the combined (with comparatively high social media presence and usage of social networks) category showed a small rise from 13.34 to 15.70 when contrasted with the high rise across categories in the mean values of BHSP test scores from 22.56 to 32.43.

Among the 162 normal category respondents in the BHSP test, 14.20% belong to the combined category of the HPD-GQ test (Fig 8.). Similarly, among the 23 clinical category respondents of the BHSP test, a very low percent of 8.7% belonged to the borderline category of the HPD-GQ test (Fig 10.). There are only 7 respondents in borderline BHSP category of which 42.86% (Fig. 9) come within the combined category of HPD-GQ test. These low percentages of risk individuals in the combined category in the different categories of BHSP test are responsible for the bleak increase of the mean value across different categories on the HPD-GQ test.

Discussion

According to DSM-5 [1], a primary symptom of NPD is impairment in self-functioning when it comes to one's identity, that is, people with NPD exhibit excessive reference to others for self-definition and self-esteem regulation. This symptom, when paired with the poor ability of NPD sufferers to handle criticism, seems to make excessive usage of social media networks such as Facebook, Twitter, etc. a potentially self-destructive platform for narcissists, as it makes them quite susceptible to criticism and realistic feedback which might affect their grandiose sense of self-importance and their inordinate fantasies of success, brilliance or beauty. The exposure to a wider audience on social media could also prove to be more censorious for narcissists, thus limiting their online activity to only slightly more than the average healthy social network user so as to seek attention and admiration, but not high enough to invite rather unpleasant consequences of social networking such as social reprobation and cyber bullying. This is the reason which accounts for the observed trends in the results.

On the other hand, we have people suffering from HPD who, according to DSM-IV-TR [5], experience significant discomfort when they are not the center of attention. The short-lived, perfunctory attention meted out to users on social media sites may, thus, prove to be unsettling for HPD sufferers. Moreover, their predilection for self-dramatization, theatricality, as well as their perception of relationships to be more intimate than they usually are, may be inconvenienced by the make-believe appearance of social interactions on virtual networks. Additionally, excessively impressionistic speech and exaggeration of emotions on social media are likely to attract criticism and mockery when they are seen to occur as frequent, repetitive patterns of user behaviour. Therefore, the prevalence of typical HPD symptoms such as seeking attention, admiration and sexually provocative behaviour might predispose a person to higher usage of social networks. However, the pitfalls above may eventually reduce their usage frequency to only slightly above the average user, as it can be seen in our results.

Conclusion

The quantification of social media usage and the discernment of rationale behind online activity for people with borderline/clinically significant NPD, HPD as well as normal healthy people reflected that those with NPD/HPD showed only a slightly above average usage of social media. The average score of the normal population for social media usage test was 13.80, whereas sufferers of NPD showed an average score of 15.83 and HPD affected population had an average score of 15.70. In a sample of 192, 20.31% were found to be suffering from narcissism, while 15.63% were detected with borderline/clinically significant HPD.

References

American Psychiatric Association (2013). *Diagnostic and Statistical Manual of Mental Disorders* (5th edition). Washington, DC: Author

Ferguson, C. J., Negy, C., (2014). Development of a brief screening questionnaire for histrionic personality 5 symptoms. *Journal of Personality and Individual Differences*, United States, In Press.

Ames, R.R., Rose, P., Anderson, C.P., (2005). The NPI-16 as a short measure of narcissism. *Journal Of Research in Personality*, 40, 440–450.

Raskin, R., & Terry, H., (1988). A principle-components analysis of the Narcissistic Personality Inventory and further evidence of its construct validity. *Journal of Personality and Social Psychology*, 54, 890–902.

Narcissistic personality disorder – Diagnostic and Statistical Manual of Mental Disorders Fourth edition Text Revision (DSM-IV-TR) *American Psychiatric Association* (2000)

Appendix

General Questionnaire (GQ)

1. What all social networking sites do you use?
    a) Facebook
    b) Instagram
    c) Twitter
    d) Snapchat
    e) Quora

2. How often do you change your profile picture on Facebook?

    a) Once/twice a week

    b) 2-4 times in 15 days

    c) Once a month

    d) 2-4 times in a year

3. How often do you update your status on FB or Tweet or both?

    a) Once/twice a week

    b) 2-4 times in 15 days

    c) Once a month

    d) 2-4 times in a year

4. How often do you tag people on FB?

    a) Once/twice a week

    b) 2-4 times in 15 days

    c) Once a month

    d) 2-4 times in a year

5. How often do you use hashtags on FB?

    a) Once/twice a week

    b) 2-4 times in 15 days

    c) Once a month

    d) 2-4 times in a year

6. How often do you check-in on FB?

    a) Once/twice a week

    b) 2-4 times in 15 days

    c) Once a month

    d) 2-4 times in a year

7. How often do you upload pictures on Instagram?

    a) Once/twice a week

    b) 2-4 times in 15 days

    c) Once a month

    d) 2-4 times in a year

8. How often do you take selfies?

    a) Once/twice a week

    b) 2-4 times in 15 days

    c) Once a month

    d) 2-4 times in a year

9. How often do you use filters or photo editing software?

    a) Once/twice a week

    b) 2-4 times in 15 days

    c) Once a month

    d) 2-4 times in a year

10. What number of likes do you usually aim for when you upload a picture on Facebook or Instagram?

    a) 0-20   b) 20-50   c) 50-100   d) >100   e) I usually do not get many likes but still I upload pictures.

11. What is your purpose when you answer any questions asked on Quora?

    a) To answer the query/ help people.

    b) Getting upvotes makes me reassured about myself.

    c) It is important for me to state my opinions.

    d) I do not answer questions on Quora.

12. Why do you like taking selfies?

    a) I like to let others know what I'm up to (Shopping, partying, etc)

    b) I think selfies are a mirror into how my life is.

    c) When I get likes on my selfies, it boosts/reaffirms my self-image.

    d) Simply because it's an ongoing trend.

13. Why would you update your relationship status on Facebook if we are to assume that you do?

    a) To let some people know if I'm taken or single.

    b) I think one needs condolences/sympathy after a break-up.

    c) I would want to make my ex-partner jealous.

    d) I would never update my relationship status no matter what.

14. Why do you usually tweet or put up a personal status on Whatsapp?

    a) I wouldn't miss a chance to express my views.

    b) I enjoy the attention these simple things can get me.

    c) My statuses/tweets indirectly serve my underlying agenda.

    d) I do not tweet/update status on Whatsapp often.

15. Which of the following is closest to your views about social media platforms such as Facebook, Instagram, Twitter, etc?

    a) I think they serve as tools to gain the admiration and attention that one deserves.

    b) I think they're a great way of being in touch with one's social circles.

    c) I think they're a great way of letting the world know what kind of person one is.

    d) I think they are overrated.

Appendix 2

Figures

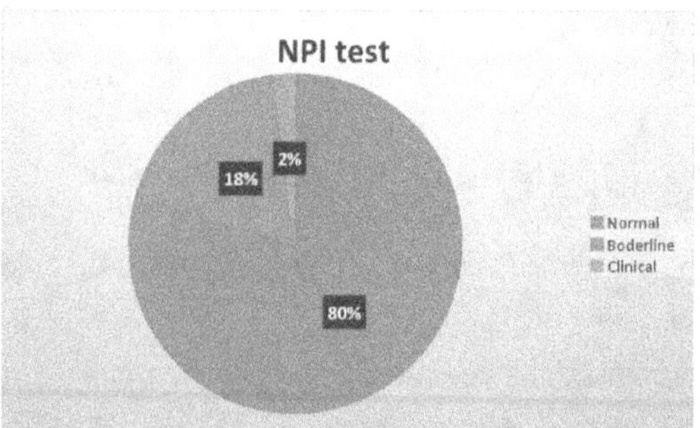

Fig 1. The pie chart shown represents the proportion of different NPI test categories for the total sample population.

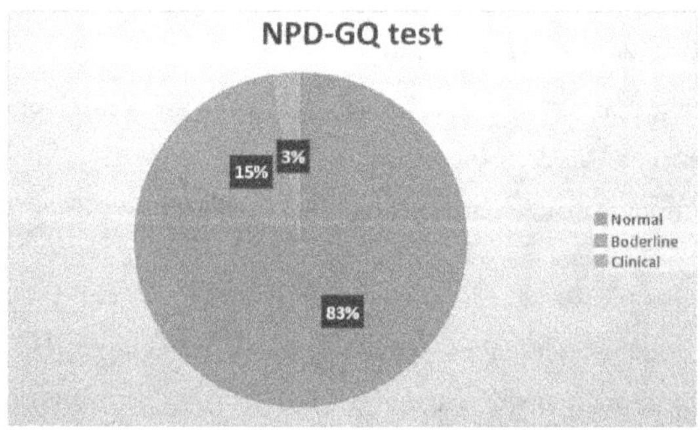

Fig 2. The pie chart shown represents the proportion of different NPD-GQ test categories for the total sample population.

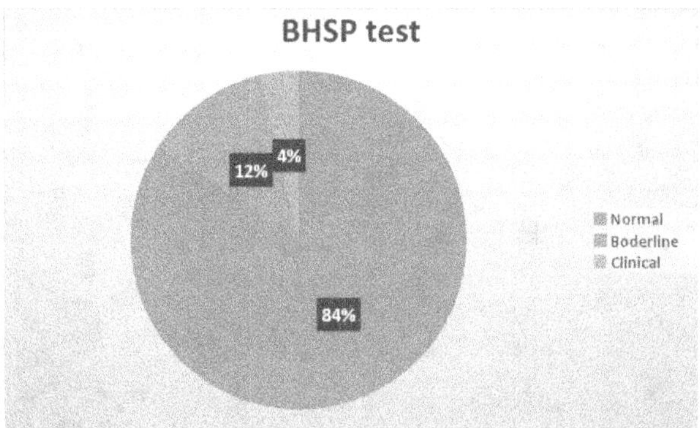

Fig 3. The pie chart shown represents the proportion of different BHSP test categories for the total sample population.

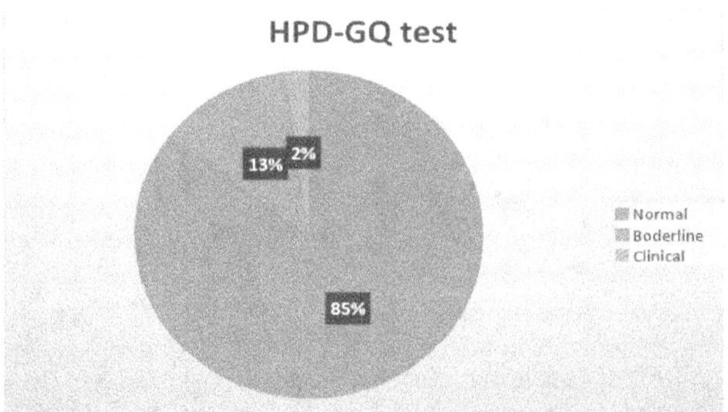

Fig 4. The pie chart shown represents the proportion of different HPD-GQ test categories for the total sample population.

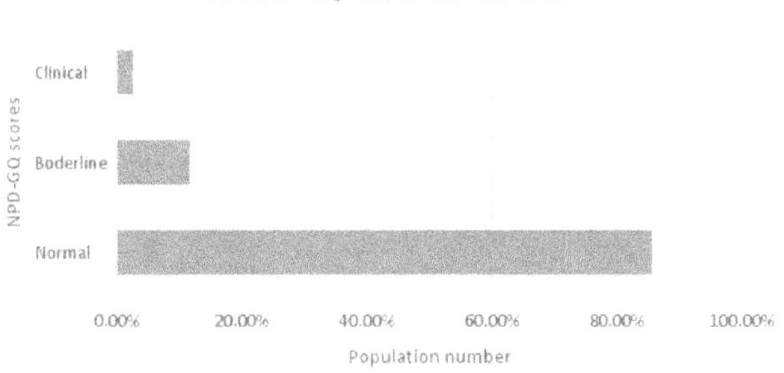

Fig 5. The bar graph shown represents the classification of Normal NPI-16 test population based on NPD-GQ test characteristics.

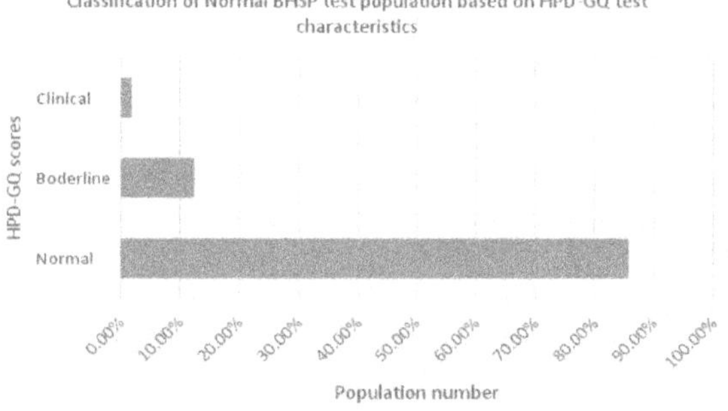

Fig 6. The bar graph shown represents the classification of Borderline NPI-16 test
population based on NPD-GQ test characteristics.

Fig 7. The bar graph shown represents the classification of Clinical NPI-16 test population
based on NPD-GQ test characteristics.

Fig 8. The pie graph shown represents the classification of Normal BHSP test population
based on HPD-GQ test characteristics.

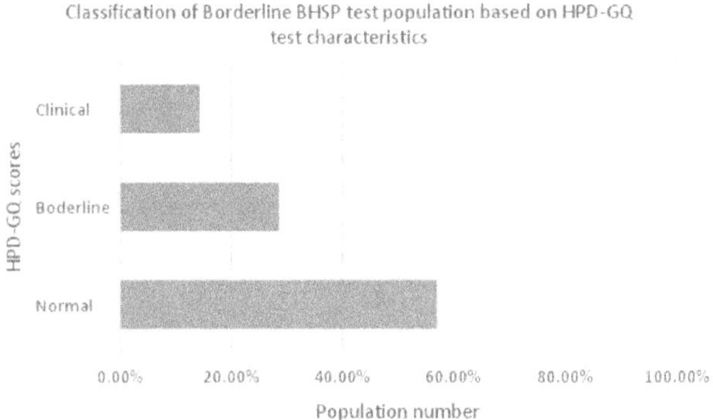

Fig 9. The pie graph shown represents the classification of Borderline BHSP test population based on HPD-GQ test characteristics.

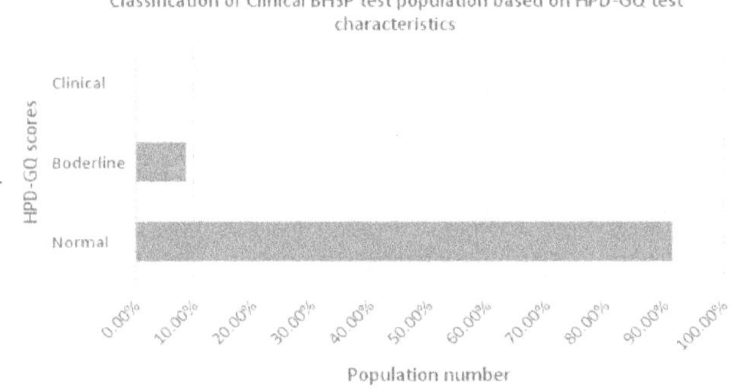

Fig 10. The bar graph shown represents the classification of Clinical BHSP test population based on HPD-GQ test characteristics.

ABOUT THE EDITORS

Zaved Ahmed Khan is a Professor at Chandigarh University, Chandigarh. For more than a decade, he has been teaching and researching in the fields of neurosciences and behavioural sciences. His interest lies in investigating the neurobiological basis for learning beahviour.

Shahila Zafar is an Assistant Professor in English at the Central University of Punjab. She has been teaching and researching for the last fifteen years. She is interested in exploring the effects of individual differences in second language learning.